Every Day with Jesus

MAR/APR 2017

The Call

'At once they left their nets and followed him.'
Mark 1:18

Selwyn Hughes
Revised and updated by Mick Brooks

© CWR 2016. Dated text previously published as *Every Day with Jesus: A Fresh Look at Discipleship* (March/April 2004) by CWR. This edition revised and updated for 2017 by Mick Brooks.

CWR, Waverley Abbey House, Waverley Lane, Farnham, Surrey GU9 8EP, UK Tel: 01252 784700
Email: mail@cwr.org.uk Registered Charity No. 294387. Registered Limited Company No. 1990308.

Cover image: Getty Images/Dougal Waters

Quiet Time image: pixabay/whatsinprague

Printed in England by Linney Print

MIX
Paper from
responsible sources
FSC® C015900

Every Day with Jesus is available in large print from CWR. It is also available on **audio and DAISY** in the UK and Eire for the sole use of those with a visual impairment worse than N12, or who are registered blind. For details please contact **Torch Trust for the Blind**, Torch House, Torch Way, Northampton Road, Market Harborough LE16 9HL. Tel: 01858 438260.

A word of introduction...

I quite like a 'top ten' list, and with Google, lists and opinions have never been easier to source – there are even websites dedicated to lists. The internet will provide an endless supply of answers for almost anything. Whether it can be trusted or is true is an entirely different matter!

There is a common entry in lists about the ten most important, world-changing moments in history: the life of Jesus Christ. There is no doubt that historians understand that this man changed the course of history and His influence and impact still continue today. Everyday people hear 'the call' and everything changes.

Calling, according to my dictionary, is a strong urge towards a particular way of life, career or vocation – or the action and sound of calling. For the early disciples and for countless men and women down the ages, the call of Christ was both. And their response to Jesus' call to 'Follow me', was not just a one-off action, but an entire lifestyle choice that changed and continually changes the world in which we live for good.

In this issue, Selwyn explores that call of Jesus and the lifelong adventure of discipleship. We discover that, like any apprenticeship, it is not always smooth, easy and untroubled. Over these next two months, we will see how Jesus lived, walked and shared His life with His early disciples and, unlike the internet, we will discover how He is entirely true and can always be trusted.

Mick Brooks, Consulting Editor

 Free small group resources to accompany this issue can be found at **www.cwr.org.uk/extra**
The *EDWJ* Facebook community is growing! To join the conversation visit **www.facebook.com/edwjpage**

A fan or a follower?

FOR READING & MEDITATION – JOHN 8:12–30

'Jesus... said, "I am the light of the world."' (v12)

The theme for this issue has been prompted by the concern that many Christians can settle for having their sins forgiven and the assurance of heaven when they die, rather than responding to Jesus' call to be a disciple – a people who follow in the steps of their Master, learn His ways and live His lifestyle. Church leaders attribute this trend to a failure to make clear to people what might be involved in following Jesus.

A large proportion of people new to faith, it seems, are being attracted to Jesus because of what He can do for them and they appear to have little interest in or understanding of what they might do for Him. One observer of contemporary church life says, 'Many of today's converts appear to follow Christ for the same reason they frequent their favourite restaurant: they both give them what they want. They love Jesus the same way they love the restaurant.'

Make no mistake: Jesus came to give us life, salvation, and the promise of heaven when we die. But there is something else: He calls us on a lifelong apprenticeship as a disciple – total commitment to Him and His cause. When we try to fit Jesus around our lives rather than our lives around Him, then whatever we may choose to call ourselves we cannot truly call ourselves 'disciples'. 'True Christianity,' says one church leader, 'is an all-out commitment to the living Christ... The Saviour is not looking for fans but followers – followers who will go with Him to death if necessary.' Those who put their own concerns first and foremost before Christ may consider themselves to be His followers but in truth they could be following another gospel.

FURTHER STUDY

Acts 2:42–47;
Gal. 1:11–17;
2:15–21

1. How did the believers demonstrate their commitment to the gospel?

2. Put into your own words Paul's commitment to Christ.

My Father and my God, my heart desires more than anything to be taken deeper into You. Help me understand all that is involved in following Your Son. Make me a true disciple. In Jesus' name. Amen.

Perspective matters

FOR READING & MEDITATION – LUKE 6:43–49

'Why do you call me, "Lord, Lord," and do not do what I say?' (v46)

Yesterday we began reflecting on the tendency to be attracted to Jesus because of what He can do for us, and the challenges in considering the implications and impact upon the lives of those He calls to follow Him. In the passage before us today, Jesus makes clear for His listeners that He anticipates more from His followers than mere lip-service. The person who says, 'Lord, Lord' but fails to do what He asks is like a man who built a house on ground without first digging foundations, says the Saviour.

FURTHER STUDY

Rom. 10:9–13; 2 Cor. 8:6–12

1. Why is it necessary to confess Jesus as Lord?

2. What perspective on giving did Paul encourage?

When I was a young man I would often hear these words: 'If you do not crown Him Lord of all, you do not crown Him Lord at all.' It is a succinct way of highlighting that unless we see our relationship to Jesus Christ as being one of commitment and trust to whatever He calls us to do and are willing to follow Him wherever He takes us, we are not really His followers at all. Our churches are filled with people who claim to be Christians yet are more concerned with pleasing themselves than pleasing the God.

A church leader reported that while he was talking to a new Christian who wanted to become a member of his church, he asked him how he was finding things in his new life. 'Fine,' said the convert, 'but I still can't come to terms with the things I have to give up.' 'Stop thinking about the things you have to give up,' said the pastor, 'and think of what Christ gave up for you.' The new Christian was stunned by this rather direct response, but it gave him a completely new perspective on the Christian life and gave him a wonderful release in his soul. Maybe some of our own patterns of thought need to be challenged in a similar manner.

Lord God, please enable me to have the right perspective on everything. Help me to focus more on what You gave up for me and less on what I am required to give up for You. Amen.

The elements of discipleship

FOR READING & MEDITATION – JOHN 1:35–51

'Come... and you will see.' (v39)

What then does being a follower of Jesus look like? Considering the word 'disciple' and the contexts in which Jesus used it will help us to more clearly understand what life is like for those who respond to His call. These meditations are devoted to examining day by day the many statements Jesus made concerning discipleship. To be a 'disciple' is to be a learner, a follower, a trained one.

Interestingly, in today's reading all the main elements of what it means to be a learner, follower and trained one of Jesus are to be seen in concentrated form. John the Baptist says to two of his disciples, 'Look, the Lamb of God!' (v35). This was the language of spiritual insight and it caused John's disciples to move their allegiance from him to Jesus. The amazing adventure of discipleship begins when we 'look' in faith to Jesus who, like the lamb in the Old Testament sacrificial system, died as our sinless substitute. And when we truly hear that call to follow Him there is an inner response from our hearts and, like Nathanael, we recognise that Jesus is our true King (v49).

So often the discipleship lifestyle is punctuated by being stopped in our tracks by Jesus, resulting in us experiencing an inward and an outward change. Jesus, for example, foretold the change that would take place in the life of Simon, Andrew's brother, when He gave him a new name which means 'rock': 'You are Simon... You will be called Cephas (which... is Peter)' (v42). Discipleship involves trusting in Christ's redemptive sacrifice, hearing His personal call, submitting to His kingly authority and experiencing an inward change. This is the true disciple's life choice.

FURTHER STUDY

1 Pet. 1:13–21; Rev. 14:1–5

1. What does Peter say discipleship involves?

2. What vision does John have of those who follow the Lamb?

Lord Jesus Christ, words are inadequate to describe how grateful I am for the times when You stop me in my tracks and call me to follow You. Help me to keep following You no matter where You take me. Amen.

The call

FOR READING & MEDITATION – MARK 1:14–20

'At once they left their nets and followed him.' (v18)

Yesterday we looked at a significant passage in which we saw Jesus calling to Him some of His first disciples. Over the next few days we shall look at similar passages, and by doing so we will profit from considering what Bible teachers describe as 'the law of first mention'. According to this principle, whenever you begin to study a topic or theme in Scripture you concentrate on the first occasion the subject is mentioned. This provides a good and reliable guide for understanding its true meaning and context.

FURTHER STUDY

Rom. 1:1–7;
1 Cor. 1:1–9

1. How does Paul view his own calling?

2. How were the Corinthians to view their calling?

The passage before us today shows how four Galilean men became Jesus' disciples as a direct result of His call. Interestingly, in ancient times it was common for would-be disciples to seek out their own masters and teachers. Jesus, however, took the initiative in summoning people to follow Him. They didn't so much seek Him; He sought them. Over and over again in the New Testament the idea is laid down that Christ's followers are people who are called. 'Brothers,' says the apostle Paul in 1 Corinthians 1:26, 'think of what you were when you were called.' We often refer to the fact that we chose Christ, and in a sense that is perfectly true. But we ought never forget that the reason we called out to Him was because He first called out to us. As an old Scottish woman put it, 'He did the courtin'.'

Christ's call, we note, overrides convention and custom, family obligations and business commitments. The sons of Zebedee left their father, their boats, and their business and, together with Simon and Andrew, set out to follow Jesus. His call upset their fishing careers but they went with Him to fish in larger waters and for a more important catch – people.

Lord Jesus, I realise that had You not called out to me I would never have called out to You. I think of what I was when I was called and what I am now. The difference is all because of You, Lord Jesus. And I am so grateful. Amen.

CWR Ministry Events

PLEASE PRAY FOR THE TEAM

DATE	EVENT	PLACE	PRESENTER(S)
3–5 Mar	Bible Discovery Weekend: Behold the Man	Waverley Abbey House	Philip Greenslade
9 Mar	Meeting Pastoral Care Challenges	WAH	Andy Peck
16 Mar	The Life and Times of Jesus	WAH	Andy Peck
21 Mar	Inspiring Women Spring Day: Living Wholeheartedly	WAH	Paula Buchel and the Inspiring Women team
23 Mar	Small Group Essentials	WAH	Andy Peck
24–26 Mar	Inspiring Women Spring Weekend: New Beginnings	WAH	Paula Buchel, Elizabeth Hodkinson and the Inspiring Women team
25 Mar	Mental Health and the Church	WAH	Mick Brooks
27–31 Mar	Introduction to Biblical Care and Counselling	Pilgrim Hall	John Munt and team
29 Mar	Great Chapters of the Bible: The Master Story	WAH	Philip Greenslade
22 Apr	Waverley Abbey College Open Day	PH	Heather Churchill, John Munt and team
22 Apr	Insight into Self-Acceptance	WAH	Chris Ledger
27 Apr	Experiencing God	WAH	Andy Peck

Please pray for our students and tutors on our ongoing BA Counselling programme at Waverley Abbey College (which takes place at Waverley Abbey House and Pilgrim Hall), as well as our Certificate in Christian Counselling and MA Counselling qualifications.

We would also appreciate prayer for our ongoing ministry in Singapore and Cambodia, as well as the many regional events that we are embarking on this year.

For further information and a full list of CWR's courses, seminars and events, call **+44 (0)1252 784719** or visit **www.cwr.org.uk/courses**

You can also download our free Prayer Track, which includes daily prayers, from **www.cwr.org.uk/free-resources**

Adherents not admirers

FOR READING & MEDITATION – MATTHEW 4:18–22

'At once they left their nets and followed him.' (v20)

This passage, a parallel to the one we looked at yesterday, brings home even more forcibly the truth that when Jesus called Peter, Andrew, James and John they left everything to follow Him. The great preacher P.T. Forsyth made the comment, slightly tongue-in-cheek no doubt, that 'Christ ruined many careers.' Yet, in reality, if we were able to speak to those whose careers Christ 'ruined' (such as Dr Martyn Lloyd Jones, who left a promising career in medicine to become a preacher), they would tell you that their careers were not so much ruined as redirected. It has to be said, of course, that Jesus does not call everyone to change his or her career. However, if He has other plans for us or if our work involves us contravening biblical principles, then He will ask us to change our job.

Jesus is not looking for admirers but adherents – not sympathisers, but men and women committed to His direction and calling. In the case of the four Galilean fishermen, it is clear that there was something so compelling about the Master that when He called them they did not hesitate to leave everything and follow Him.

Permit a personal question: would you be willing to give up everything in response to Christ's call? As I once heard it put, 'Christ does not ask everyone to give up everything for Him but He does expect them to be willing to give up everything.' Jesus has always been clear, from the very beginning, concerning the cost of discipleship. So we too as His ambassadors and representatives need also to be clear about what it means to follow Him. Jesus never misled people when He called them to faith in Him. Neither must we.

FURTHER STUDY

Acts 4:32–37;
Phil. 3:3–11

1. What were the early believers prepared to give up?

2. What did the apostle Paul give up?

My Father and my God, help me, I pray, not to hold anything back or withdraw from any commitment I have made. I long to fully trust You, be fully surrendered to You and be fully Yours. In Jesus' name. Amen.

Newness – a must

FOR READING & MEDITATION – LUKE 5:1–11

*'Simon Peter... fell at Jesus' knees and said, "Go away from me, Lord;
I am a sinful man!"' (v8)*

We continue studying Jesus' encounters with His first disciples in order to understand more deeply the roots of discipleship. Luke's account of Jesus' calling of the disciples focuses mainly on Simon Peter. Picture the scene with me.

The Saviour had been speaking by the Sea of Galilee. As the crowd pressed towards Him, eager to hear His words of wisdom, He got into Simon Peter's boat, sat down, and continued teaching. When He finished He turned to Peter and said, 'Put out into deep water, and let down the nets for a catch' (v4). That must have struck Peter as rather odd, don't you think, especially as Jesus' trade was carpentry, not fishing? Peter explained that he had fished all night and caught nothing but, at Jesus' command, he did not hesitate to do as he had been told. Instantly, the fish that had been eluding him all night suddenly filled his nets, so much so that the nets began to break. Clearly this was something beyond the ordinary. Simon Peter had witnessed an amazing miracle.

And what was his response? He turned to Jesus and said, 'Go away from me, Lord; I am a sinful man!' There was something about Jesus' moral majesty that revealed, by contrast, the guilt and sin in Simon Peter's heart. Doubtless it dawned upon him that contact with Jesus means that one does not stay the same person but begins on a new path. Something radical took place in the heart of Simon Peter that moment which led him from fishing in the comparative isolation of the Sea of Galilee to fishing for people in the ocean of the world. That call to discipleship involves newness – becoming a new person and walking a new path.

FURTHER STUDY

Acts 5:17–21, 27–32;
Rom. 6:1–7;
7:4–6;
2 Cor. 5:14–21

1. What is Peter's message of this new life?

2. Where does Paul say this newness comes from?

Lord Jesus, how can I thank You enough for making me a new person, giving me a new nature and promising that one day I will even have a new name? I am grateful beyond words. Amen.

A taxman's transformation

FOR READING & MEDITATION – MARK 2:13–17

'"Follow me," Jesus told him, and Levi got up and followed him.' (v14)

Taxmen are often characterised as some of the most unpopular people on earth. All the more so in the time of Jesus. Levi, the tax gatherer, put himself in a strategic spot in Capernaum so as to collect the taxes of those going to and from Galilee. Capernaum was the crossing point between the territory governed by Antipas and that governed by one of Herod the Great's other sons – Philip. Missing no opportunity to raise revenues, these local lords, backed by the occupying Romans, exacted tolls on anyone entering their domain.

FURTHER STUDY

Acts 16:22–34;
1 Tim. 1:12–17

1. Why was the Philippian jailer filled with joy?

2. Why was Paul so grateful?

Tax collectors were the victims of much abuse and were used to people either shouting at them or cursing them as they grudgingly paid their taxes. One day Jesus came along, stopped at Levi's booth, looked him in the eyes and simply said, 'Follow me.' Immediately he got up and followed Jesus. What happened to the money he had collected? Who would replace him? Was he under contract? These questions lie unanswered. We can be sure, however, that Jesus would not have encouraged Levi to do anything inappropriate or irresponsible.

Once again this example highlights that when Jesus calls He anticipates a response of a life given in relationship and trust. Dietrich Bonhoeffer, the German pastor who was executed by the Nazis just before the end of World War II, said, 'Had Levi stayed at his post, Jesus would have been his present help in time of trouble, but not the Lord of his whole life.' Levi sensed that he was being called by a higher authority than Antipas and a greater king than Caesar. He might have been unpopular with the people but Jesus called him to be one of His disciples. Are we, I wonder, willing to respond to such a call as that?

Jesus, how glad I am that Your call came also to me. It was a call that overwhelmed all my suspicions and conquered my heart's antipathy. Again I am truly grateful. Eternally grateful. Amen.

Jesus – boundary breaker

FOR READING & MEDITATION – MATTHEW 9:9–13

'the Pharisees... asked his disciples, "Why does your teacher eat with tax collectors and 'sinners'?"' (v11)

Today's passage parallels the one we considered yesterday. Matthew and Levi are really one and the same person. We reflect on the call of Levi, or Matthew, again today because Matthew's Gospel brings out a particular emphasis not found in Mark's account.

We are told that Jesus had dinner at Matthew's house in company with 'many tax collectors and "sinners"' (v10). Tax collectors were regarded by most people in Israel as the dregs of society because they colluded with the Romans. But what does the term 'sinners' mean in this passage? It is generally thought that here 'sinners' is used of a special class of people in Israel who had gone outside the acceptable boundaries of the Jewish religion. They had either failed or refused to practise the rituals of the Jewish faith. When Jesus sat down with such 'sinners' He was heavily criticised by the Pharisees, for they were keen to restore Israel to what they believed to be the true standards of Old Testament teaching. In doing so, the circle of who was accepted as a genuine member of God's covenant people became tighter and tighter with many excluded.

FURTHER STUDY

Jer. 7:1–11;
1 John 1:5–10

1. Who did Jeremiah say was acceptable to God?

2. What is given to those who acknowledge their sin?

Jesus, however, was a 'boundary breaker'. His way of restoring the nation of Israel spiritually was to start with those who heeded His call and committed themselves to Him. When Jesus was alerted to what the Pharisees were saying about Him He declared, 'It is not the healthy who need a doctor, but the sick' (v12). The Pharisees were in the same condition as the taxmen and 'sinners' when it came to the matter of the heart. It is sad that they failed to recognise that fact, for we can change only that which we acknowledge.

My Father and my God, how thankful I am that You have sought me out even in my 'sinfulness'. This has led to such great changes in my life. All honour and glory be to Your peerless and precious name. Amen.

Why twelve?

FOR READING & MEDITATION – MATTHEW 10:1–4

'He called his twelve disciples to him and gave them authority to drive out evil spirits and to heal' (v1)

Jesus, as we know, gathered the Twelve around Him to be His first disciples. We do not have the details of how every single one was called, but there can be little doubt that each was personally sought out and called by Jesus.

The question is often asked when considering the number of disciples Jesus chose: why twelve? Was it just a random figure plucked out of the air or was there some deep meaning behind His choice of twelve? The number twelve would have carried for the Jews of Jesus' day a special significance. They would have known that the nation of Israel had been born of twelve tribes, and so thoughtful Israelites would not have been left in doubt as to the importance of Christ's selection of twelve men to form His ministry team. He was symbolically reassigning the leadership of the people of God to artisans and fishermen!

FURTHER STUDY

Eph. 2:12–22;
Rev. 21:5–14

1. Who make up the members of God's household?

2. How does John describe the holy city, Jerusalem?

What an outstanding act of authority this was. Those who had the insight to see the Saviour's strategy must have been astonished by it. The Twelve had been chosen to form the nucleus of a new and restored people of God. Who but God could do such a thing? Later these ordinary men chosen by Jesus to be His disciples became apostles and helped to lay down the doctrinal foundation on which the Church of Jesus Christ was built and on which a whole new covenant family was created. The Twelve had a mixture of personalities and at times their temperaments clashed. Yet ultimately, under Jesus' masterly supervision and guidance, and with one sad exception, all of them became the men God intended them to be. One has only to think, as an example, of how volatile, unpredictable Peter became a solid rock in the early Church.

Lord Jesus, how wonderful it is that You gather men and women with so many differences of personality and temperament and they become followers with one purpose. I count myself happy to be amongst them. Thank You, dear Saviour. Amen.

Helping people worldwide

CWR regularly receives requests from people all over the world who want to receive counselling training. The need for training in counselling and people helping skills is great in places such as Cambodia, Kenya, Singapore and Brunei, and this need continues to grow.

It is clear that God is guiding CWR to invest more time and effort into international ministry, but this can only be made possible by God's grace and your generosity and support.

'This is a wonderful course that is not just helping me to help others, but has helped me evaluate my own life and past. A really precious course that is very impactful.'
– 2016 counselling course delegate, Cambodia

Please help us to bless these countries that are calling out for teaching, resources and support, and help more people experience personal transformation through CWR's counselling training.

If you would like to prayerfully make a donation to our work around the world, please fill in the 'Gift to CWR' section on the order form at the back of these notes, completing the Gift Aid declaration if appropriate. Or visit **www.cwr.org.uk/donate**

Plugged into truth

FOR READING & MEDITATION – JOHN 6:60–71

'On hearing it, many of his disciples said, "This is a hard teaching. Who can accept it?"' (v60)

Having looked over the past days at how Jesus called together His first disciples, we move on now to consider His approach to those outside of the Twelve whom He also called to become His followers.

It seems clear from the Gospels that many were attracted to Jesus not just because of His words but also because of His ability to work miracles. No doubt the miracle recorded in the earlier part of John 6 – the feeding of the five thousand – led many to possibly think: if we follow this man He can give us bread and we will not have to work for it. If this was the kind of thinking going on in people's minds you can be sure that Jesus was well aware of it. That is probably why He would often prick the bubble of applause with statements intended to cause people to consider carefully what it meant to follow Him. News of the miracle of the feeding of the five thousand spread like wildfire, and in the passage before us now we hear Jesus saying some challenging things to the people, so much so that we read: 'From this time many of his disciples turned back and no longer followed him' (v66).

One thing is clear about His approach to recruiting His followers: He never sold them short. The Saviour always told it as it was. Jesus was well aware that there were many fair-weather followers in the crowds that gathered to listen to Him, who wanted to see what they could get rather than what they could give. Few were willing to enter into a long-term commitment to Him and put Him before everyone and everything. It is one thing to be caught up with the electric atmosphere that surrounds Jesus but it's quite another to be plugged into the truth.

FURTHER STUDY

Phil. 4:14–20; 3 John 1–12

1. For what commitment does Paul commend the Philippians?

2. In what ways is Gaius plugged into the truth?

Gracious God and loving heavenly Father, save me, I pray, from becoming a fair-weather follower of Your Son. If You are calling me to a deeper commitment, then help me respond to that challenge. In Jesus' name I pray. Amen.

A true follower's heartbeat

FOR READING & MEDITATION – JOHN 2:12–25

'But Jesus would not entrust himself to them, for he knew all men.'
(v24)

Yesterday we explored how Jesus knew in His heart that some were drawn to Him not because of His message but because of His miracles. This is made clear in the passage before us now.

When Jesus came to Jerusalem and saw the Temple being desecrated, He took a whip and drove out the sheep and cattle and overturned the tables of the money-changers. Following that, He continued to stay in Jerusalem and work many miracles. Many, we are told, 'believed in his name' (v23). But then we read these interesting words: 'Jesus would not entrust himself to them, for he knew all men.' The Saviour knew full well how fragile was the people's interest in Him and how changeable were their feelings. He saw deep into the human heart and was completely aware that the admiration of the crowd and celebrity status they gave Him could quickly change. It may not have been the same crowd that later in His life cried for Him to be crucified but it was the same human nature. People are perfectly capable of wanting to give Christ a crown today and a cross tomorrow.

How capricious is the human heart. Just as in New Testament times, so now there are those who join the Church in the hope that their needs will be met by Christ – for instance, the need for increased finances, for healing, or for employment. Then, when things don't go the way they expect, they turn away from Him as quickly as they turned towards Him. Jesus may well answer prayers of people for the things we have mentioned (and often does) but the heartbeat of Jesus' true followers is a relationship that is not dependent on Him meeting our expectations but one that seeks to meet His.

FURTHER STUDY

John 6:60–71;
Acts 8:9–13,
18–23

1. Why did some disciples desert Jesus and others not?

2. What was wrong with Simon's response?

Lord Jesus, forgive me if I regard my expectations of You as being more important than Your expectations of me. I know You delight in answering prayer but not always in the way I expect. Help me to accept that – to trust You no matter what. Amen.

Counting the cost

FOR READING & MEDITATION – MATTHEW 8:18–22

'Jesus replied, "Foxes have holes and birds of the air have nests, but the Son of Man has nowhere to lay his head."' (v20)

Even the most casual reader of the Gospels cannot help but notice that Jesus never missed an opportunity to make clear to people the cost of being one of His disciples. The Saviour never disguised the fact that there is a price to be paid if we follow Him. He was relentlessly realistic in spelling out the possible consequences of coming over onto His side.

In today's passage Jesus makes clear to a would-be disciple the possible cost to be considered in following Him. Any evangelism that plays down the cost of discipleship betrays Jesus. Dietrich Bonhoeffer called this 'cheap grace'. We cannot smooth away the rough edges of the cross for the sake of gaining easy converts. Nor can we attempt a road-widening scheme on the 'narrow… road that leads to life' (Matt. 7:14) in order to make the gospel more accessible to people of any generation. Discipleship is always on His terms, not ours.

FURTHER STUDY

John 3:1–10,
16–18;
21:18–19;
Acts 9:11–19

1. What terms of discipleship did Jesus spell out for Nicodemus?

2. What cost did both Peter and Paul face?

Sometimes the gospel is presented in our churches in ways that remind one of a free trip to Disneyland. 'Come to Jesus', certain preachers say, 'and all your troubles will be over.' Really? Many find that when they come to Jesus they have more troubles than they had before. A large number of Christians will tell you that when they became believers they found that their families and friends ignored them; they were ridiculed and in some cases disinherited for the sake of the gospel. Some have even found misunderstanding in their closest relationships because of their commitment to the Saviour. It is always best in the long run to make clear to new Christians that there is a cost to knowing Jesus.

Gracious God, forgive us that so often in our eagerness to win people to You we hype up Your gospel and sugar-coat its costs. Help us be honest in everything we do for You, especially our evangelism. In Jesus' name. Amen.

'Evanjellybabies'

FOR READING & MEDITATION – LUKE 9:57–62

*'Jesus replied, "No-one who puts his hand to the plough and looks
back is fit for service in the kingdom of God."' (v62)*

This passage, which sheds more light than yesterday's, presents even more clearly the need for honesty when sharing with people what is involved in following Christ.

The account shows us three men who wanted to follow Jesus. Eugene Peterson, in *The Message*, captures the force of what Jesus had to say to each of them. To the man who said, 'I will follow you wherever you go,' He gave this somewhat blunt reply: 'Are you ready to rough it? We're not staying in the best inns, you know.' To the man who claimed he had to first go and bury his father Jesus said, 'First things first. Your business is life, not death. And life is urgent: Announce God's kingdom!' And to the man who said that he had to straighten things out at home before committing himself to becoming a disciple Jesus said, 'No procrastination. No backward looks. You can't put God's kingdom off till tomorrow. Seize the day.'

FURTHER STUDY

Acts 9:19–28;
Col. 3:1–10

1. In what ways did Saul seize the day?

2. How did Paul exhort the Colossians to put first things first?

Significantly, Luke notes that this happened 'as they were walking along the road' (v57). The road on which they were walking led to Jerusalem – the place where Jesus would be put to death. To follow Him on that road is not always a rosy prospect. One church leader said – and there is little doubt he is right – that if we were as honest as Jesus was when presenting the gospel and made clear the cost of discipleship, we might well have fewer converts but the ones we had would be true disciples. Much of today's evangelism softens the cost of answering His call, of sugar-coating the gospel to make it more palatable. Someone has described this kind of evangelism as 'evanjellyism' which produces only 'evanjellybabies' – people who bend easily in the moment of testing.

Lord Jesus, while we can never accuse You of mis-selling the gospel, sometimes in our eagerness to win people to You we come very close to doing that. Help us be clear and balanced when calling people to commitment. Amen.

A dawn but no sunset

FOR READING & MEDITATION – MARK 2:18–22

'How can the guests of the bridegroom fast while he is with them?
They cannot, so long as they have him with them.' (v19)

The people who questioned Jesus about fasting must have been quite surprised by His answer, especially if they were of the religiously legalistic type. Eugene Peterson paraphrases Jesus' reply in this way: 'When you're celebrating a wedding, you don't skimp on the cake and wine. You feast. Later you may need to pull in your belt, but not now. As long as the bride and groom are with you, you have a good time.' On the surface Jesus' words appear to disparage the practice of fasting, but we know from other statements He made (Matt. 6:17, for example) this was not so. John's disciples may have been fasting as an expression of repentance intended to hasten the coming of the Messiah, whereas the Pharisees often fasted in order to impress people with their spirituality.

FURTHER STUDY

Rom. 14:16–17;
Phil. 1:3–11,
14–19;
1 Pet. 1:1–9

1. What made Paul rejoice?

2. What gives joy to those who believe?

Jesus explained that in His Person the kingdom of God was already present, and the image He chose to illustrate that a Jewish wedding – an event that sometimes lasted a whole week and was always full of joy. I believe He is saying that fasting is not appropriate when the circumstances call for feasting. And you can't easily mix the old with the new either. If you sew a patch of new fabric onto old cloth to cover a hole, the fabric will shrink and tear away, making matters worse. Similarly, if you try to contain fizzing new wine in old wineskins, the old skins will burst under the strain.

Jesus used these figures of speech to show that His coming to this world was a time for breaking with the old and ushering in the new. When the sun comes up, what need is there of candles? To be a disciple of Jesus is to be part of a dawn which will never end in a sunset. Hallelujah!

Lord Jesus, once again, I thank You that You have called me to participate in this revolution which You brought to the world. My gratitude is Yours for ever. Amen.

Not a spectator sport!

FOR READING & MEDITATION – MATTHEW 9:35–38

'Jesus went through all the towns and villages, teaching in their synagogues, preaching the good news of the kingdom' (v35)

What an amazing time it must have been when Jesus was here on earth and the first waves of the kingdom of God broke upon the shores of this tired world. Good news, never before heralded, is brought to weary and disconsolate men and women. Sickness and disease gives way to the power that flows from God to the infirm and afflicted. Today's passage, brief though it is, records how God's truth was preached with heart-stopping authority.

To be called by Jesus is far more than to be someone who has made 'a decision for Christ' or been 'smitten with religion'; a disciple is someone who has become involved in a glorious revolution. In the words of theologians Glen Stassen and David Gushee: 'Jesus taught that as His disciples obey Him and practice what He taught and lived, they participate in the reign of God that Jesus inaugurated during His earthly ministry, and that will reach its climax when He comes again.' Even though we are not literally walking with Jesus in the way the first disciples did, it remains true that Christians are those whose everyday lives are being used to bring God's saving rule to the world.

Discipleship is not a spectator sport! We become caught up in the feelings and desires that flow through the heart of the Trinity. We long that lost sheep will find the Shepherd, that workers will be sent into the harvest, and that injustice will be put right. Sharing the compassion of God, we find that not only do our hearts ache over a lost world but that He works through us to make us part of the answer. Disciples are people who not only share their Master's feelings but are used by Him in working out His purposes.

FURTHER STUDY

Luke 10:1–11; Acts 14:1–4, 8–17

1. How did Jesus' disciples participate in the reign of God?

2. How were Paul and Barnabas caught up in God's plans?

Lord Jesus Christ, the more I realise that I am a participant in Your plan to bring Your saving rule to the world, the more my heart yearns to show its gratitude. May I do so not only with my lips but also with my life. For Your name's sake. Amen.

'Under instruction'

FOR READING & MEDITATION – MATTHEW 10:5–25

'A student is not above his teacher, nor a servant above his master.'
(v24)

In the chapter before us today Jesus spelt out in the clearest fashion His expectations of those who have chosen to follow Him. As He sent out the Twelve, He gave them instructions on how to represent Him and His kingdom before the people they would meet. In today's text, He makes clear that a student is not above his teacher, nor a servant above his master. Disciples need always to remember that this relationship is a permanent state of affairs. We never rise above the Master and Teacher so as to dictate to Him. In Christ's school of discipleship no one ever graduates with a 'Master's Degree'!

FURTHER STUDY

Acts 14:19–28;
1 Pet. 2:18–25

1. Notice how Paul and Barnabas display long-term commitment.

2. How did Peter encourage slaves to follow in Christ's steps?

When the famous Watchman Nee came to the UK in the 1930s, he was fascinated to see that learner drivers displayed an 'L-plate' on their cars. This conspicuous red letter 'L' on a white background tells everyone that the driver is under instruction. Disciples are always 'under instruction'. At best we can aspire to be like our Master and Teacher; we will most certainly never reach the stage where we no longer need to be instructed by Him.

When disciples become *like* their Master they may well find themselves being treated as He was treated by those whose personal position and power is threatened by the message of the kingdom. Jesus drew the scorn of those whose godless lifestyle He challenged, and we can expect similar treatment when we do the same. As His disciples, we share His companionship and leadership, and we may also share His fate – rejection, opposition, misunderstanding, ostracism, perhaps even death. No matter what, He will never leave us, and no matter what, may we never leave Him.

Father God, help me understand that to be Your disciple means I am in the faith for the long haul. There is to be no turning back. I'm in this no matter what. I'm Yours all the way. Amen.

No secret disciples

FOR READING & MEDITATION – MATTHEW 10:26–32

*'So do not be afraid of them. There is nothing concealed that will not
be disclosed, or hidden that will not be made known.' (v26)*

It is often said that the most frequent exhortation in Scripture
is not 'Do not sin' but 'Do not be afraid'. This is just what
Jesus urged and reminded His disciples in the verses before us
today. The reason He gave, however, seems somewhat strange.
'Nothing will remain concealed,' He told them, 'but all will be
disclosed.' How was that to help them not to fear?

Jesus was saying that one day everything about Him would
be out in the open and the whole world will know that He is the
one true Lord and Saviour. The knowledge that our Jesus is in
charge and that His will for the universe is ultimately
going to prevail ought to disperse every fear in our
heart. For that reason alone there is no need to fear
going public now. Jesus does not want us to be secret
disciples. What greater incentive do we need to live
faithfully and fearlessly for Him than to know we are
part of a cause that will ultimately prevail?

FURTHER STUDY

Phil. 2:5–11;
1 Pet. 3:8–18;
Rev. 1:4–8

1. What will
happen when
everything
about Jesus is
out in the open?

2. How does
Peter suggest
we overcome
fear?

Having told His disciples that they need not be
afraid, Jesus then went on to warn them that there
is Someone of whom they should be afraid: 'But
rather fear Him who is able to destroy both soul and
body in hell' (v28, NKJV). Commentators differ as to
whether Jesus was talking here about God or the evil
one. However the thrust of the passage implies that
though we may fear the devil in the same way we exercise
caution in crossing a road, the One whom we should have
fear and reverence for is the One who can destroy both soul
and body in hell. Yet, at the same time, for the disciple, this
reverence for God is combined with a trust in a loving Father
who is concerned about the smallest details of our lives.

**Loving Lord, help me absorb this truth that ultimately Your cause
will prevail throughout the whole universe. Nothing is outside Your
love and care, so I need never be afraid of what happens to me. I
am so thankful. Amen.**

'Insider knowledge'

FOR READING & MEDITATION – MATTHEW 11:25–27

'I praise you, Father... because you have hidden these things from the wise and learned, and revealed them to little children.' (v25)

Followers of Jesus are the most privileged people in the universe. We are privy to things that others struggle to understand. The Father, we are told, has revealed the mysteries of His kingdom, not to the worldly wise and the intellectually great but to 'little children'. It may not be flattering to be called 'little children' but the fact is that the truths of the kingdom cannot be discovered through intellectual probing alone but by revelation. If they were not revealed to us then we would never understand them, since worldly knowledge and wisdom cannot lead us to them. First we come to know Jesus and then we come to know all about the kingdom. It just doesn't work the other way round.

FURTHER STUDY

1 Cor. 1:26–31; 2:6–12; Eph. 3:2–12

1. In whom should we boast and why?

2. What, according to Paul, is hidden and what is revealed?

There is nothing little children like more than to snuggle up to their father or mother and be told a secret! Those who try to figure out the truth about Jesus and His kingdom simply by using their intellectual ability are unlikely to progress very far. But when they come to Christ in the attitude of childlike trust and receive Him into their hearts as their Saviour, then that humble dependency opens them up to seeing and understanding things they could never glean through intellectual reasoning alone.

Self-assured intellectuals just don't 'get it' when it comes to understanding the things of God. They will never comprehend, without the operation of divine grace on the heart, that this Galilean carpenter, Jesus of Nazareth, is none other than the Son of God to whom God has entrusted 'all things'. As such, He has a unique 'inside knowledge' of His Father which He shares with His disciples. As we said – Jesus' followers are the most privileged people in the universe.

Heavenly Father, there are just not enough words to express my appreciation that you have revealed to me the truths of Your kingdom. Why I should be chosen for this privilege is beyond me. But I shall rejoice in it now and through all eternity. Amen.

Homesickness

FOR READING & MEDITATION – MATTHEW 11:28–29

*'Come to me, all you who are weary and burdened,
and I will give you rest.' (v28)*

C alvin Miller, in his wonderful allegory of Jesus' life entitled *The Singer*, intriguingly suggests that Jesus was singing a song no one else knew. What was even more shocking was that those who professed to be well versed in the knowledge of God showed no desire at all to learn His tune. Only the 'little ones' – the least, the last, and the lost, the tax collectors and 'sinners', the sick and the poor – seemed to understand the enchanting melodies He sang. And the more they followed Him and listened to Him and felt His loving acceptance, the more they heard in Him the music of eternity.

It is the purpose of God to restore fallen human beings into fellowship with Himself. Someone has commented, 'There is only one sickness – homesickness.' Those outside of the kingdom, whether they realise it or not, are homesick. They have one foot in time and one foot in eternity, and they are not at home in either. In fact, they are afraid of both. They are afraid because they can't put the two together and, in trying to make sense of things, live a restless existence here on earth.

Discipleship may involve laying things down, but we gain something far more valuable through Christ – rest. Those who are prepared to take His yoke upon themselves and join themselves to Him may think they are burdening themselves with religious obligation, but in reality they discover that His yoke is no more a burden than wings are to a bird. When the soul commits itself to God, it finds what it has always longed for – perfect peace and rest. As St Augustine discovered: 'Our hearts are restless until they find their rest in Thee.'

FURTHER STUDY

Phil. 4:4–9;
1 John 5:1–12

1. How does Paul echo the words of Jesus?

2. How does John highlight the unity of the Father, Son and Spirit?

Father, I am so glad that I have found my way home. But when I realise that there are so many who have not yet found that way, my heart aches. May many this day, all over the world, discover the joy of homecoming. In Jesus' name I pray. Amen.

Discover God's story

Knowing how to approach the Bible can feel daunting. Is it a kind of spiritual directory? Do we just stick with our favourite passages? Or is the Bible essentially a narrative of God's dealings with His world? Understanding the Bible as *God's story* transforms our relationship with Him, and the way in which we live our lives each day. This year, come to a seven-day series, which will explore this vital topic. CWR tutor and course leader Philip Greenslade introduces **Living Out of God's Story**.

Tell us a little about the background behind this exciting new course.
CWR have previously run a course called The Big Story, which examined some of the interweaving narratives and themes of the Bible. This new extended course intends to show how each stage of God's covenantal revelation has ethical and social implications for all of us today.

What are the aims of this new course?
First, the course offers a concise summary of God's saving story, tracing its key covenantal stages. It makes the case that by conversion we are drawn by grace into this story, and by faith become believing participants in it. Second, the course encourages us to learn to live *in* the story, by understanding what it is, where it's going, how we interact with others, and how our Christian character develops as we faithfully play our part.

nd how you can play a part

In this way we may learn to live *out of* the story, responding wisely and biblically to the social and ethical challenges we face today. This will shape our views of freedom, authority, social justice and what it means to be a human being in God's image. It may also help us learn how to 'improvise' when faced with issues not mentioned directly in Scripture.

Who would benefit from this course and what can they expect?
Anyone interested in deepening their understanding of God's Word would benefit! This includes group leaders, youth leaders, counsellors, pastors, storytellers, evangelists and many more. Even if you have attended The Big Story in the past, this course focuses on how our knowledge and understanding of the Bible affects how we live it out. So anyone with an interest in biblical ethics should come along, too. People can expect to discover how we can live counter-culturally in the confidence that the biblical world-view offers a cohesive explanation of reality. As we do, we begin to understand our own place in God's master story.

Living Out of God's Story

Led by Philip Greenslade and Andy Peck
Wed 3, 10, 17, 24 May and 7, 14, 21 June
at Waverley Abbey House
To find out more and to book,
visit **www.cwr.org.uk/courses**

Breaking more boundaries

FOR READING & MEDITATION – LUKE 8:1–3

'These women were helping to support them out of their own means.' (v3)

Although Jesus called twelve men to be His disciples, He nevertheless readily accepted women into His immediate circle also. In fact, they became His closest friends. Joanna, the wife of Chuza, the manager of Herod's household, was just one of several women who supported His ministry and who almost certainly put both their money and their homes at His disposal. They took enormous social risks in doing this, but doubtless His words had struck home to such a degree that they were willing to give up everything to follow Him.

We can be sure that Jesus, being who He was, would never have taken advantage of any woman's or anyone's generosity.

Previously we said Jesus was a 'boundary breaker' and this was certainly true in His relationships with women. Of course, He never overstepped the bounds of propriety ordained by God but He did take many cultural risks in breaching social and traditional conventions to display God's respect and concern for women. Israel at that time was a strongly patriarchal society, and even to stop and talk to a woman – as Jesus did with the 'woman at the well' (see John 4) – broke normal conventions. We can well imagine what gossiping tongues said about the fact that Jesus attracted women to His cause. But that did not deter Him. It was right to treat women as equal to men, and Jesus never failed to do that which was right, even when it went completely against the social customs of His day. Over the centuries, the Church, generally speaking, has not earned itself a good record as regards its treatment of women. One thing is certain: it has not got its poor attitude to women from Jesus.

FURTHER STUDY

Acts 12:5, 11–14; 16:11–15,40; Rom. 16:1–16

1. What part did women play in the life of the Early Church?

2. For what did Paul commend women in the church at Rome?

Lord Jesus, help us, we who follow in Your footsteps, to be 'boundary breakers' too. Whenever we come across a custom that clearly is contrary to Your will, give us the courage to do the right thing. Amen.

No greater family

FOR READING & MEDITATION – MARK 3:31–35

'Whoever does God's will is my brother and sister and mother.' (v35)

If Jesus' respect for the dignity of women caused some people to be astonished, then His attitude to His own natural family must have produced a similar reaction.

In the modern Western world we are used to having our family dispersed, with siblings and children in far-flung places, living independent lives. But in Eastern societies, then as now, things were very different. The family was/is a close-knit unit – an extended group of people of all ages living in close proximity to each other and supporting each other financially and emotionally. To threaten this would cause quite a stir. But here Jesus appears to put the claims of the kingdom before family loyalty. In response to the news that His mother and brothers were outside, Jesus looked around and said to everyone within the sound of His voice: 'Right here, right in front of you – my mother and my brothers. Obedience is thicker than blood' (*The Message*).

This, however, should not be regarded as an attack upon the family. Far from it. Jesus reserved strong words for those who neglected their family obligations under the guise of religious duty. Nevertheless, He was placing the family in the larger context of the claims of God's kingdom. A new day was dawning. No one could escape its challenge by hiding behind domestic conventions. It was time to decide whether or not to do the will of God. Jesus was creating a new covenant family for His Father, and every allegiance – whether family, tribal or national – takes second place to this. Visit a Christian church anywhere in the world and you will find yourself part of a family. There is no greater family than the family of God.

FURTHER STUDY

Gal. 3:26–29;
Col. 3:11;
1 Pet. 1:22–2:6

1. How does Paul describe God's new covenant family?

2. What kind of family does Peter describe?

My Father and my God, I am so glad that now I am in Christ I belong to everyone else who is in Christ. Though I am thankful for my earthly family, I am even more grateful for the wider family with whom I am destined to spend eternity. Amen.

The point of the parables

FOR READING & MEDITATION – MARK 4:1–12

'Then Jesus said, "He who has ears to hear, let him hear."' (v9)

The contrast between Christ's 'little children' and those who think they understand the Christian message by intellect alone becomes apparent once again, as Jesus explained the reason behind His parables to the disciples.

What Jesus actually says contradicts the commonly held view that He spoke in parables to make it easy for us to understand the truth. Parables, we are told, are like illustrations preachers use to help make their message clear. But this seems to be the exact opposite of the case as Jesus presents it here.

FURTHER STUDY

2 Sam. 12: 1–10,13; Acts 11:1–12

1. How did Nathan's parable get past David's mental defences?

2. What means did God employ to slip past Peter's defences?

Jesus spoke in parables not to simplify the truth of the kingdom but almost, it seems, to conceal it from those who resisted God's claims upon them. The NIV Study Bible states that the words 'so that' found in verse 12 show 'Jesus likens His preaching in parables to the ministry of Isaiah, which, while it gained some disciples (Isa. 8:16), was also to expose the hard-hearted resistance of the many to God's warning and appeal.' Parables have another purpose also: they are designed to tease, challenge, and get behind our mental defences. They are intended to make us ask 'What does that mean?' or 'What can He be getting at?' or even 'How dare He say that?'

The parables Jesus told were understood only by those who wanted to know the truth. Understanding His illustrations was not so much a matter of the head as of the heart. Often Jesus would tell parables and then walk away without explanation. Eugene Peterson says: 'Parables aren't illustrations that make things easier; they make things harder by requiring the exercise of our imaginations which, if we aren't careful, becomes the exercise of faith.'

My Father and my God, how glad I am that by Your Holy Spirit You found a way to slip past my defences and invade my soul with the truth about Jesus. Now I find myself a new person in a new world. Thank You, my Father. Amen.

A friendly invasion

FOR READING & MEDITATION – MARK 4:30–34

'He did not say anything to them without using a parable.' (v34)

There is little doubt that Jesus' favourite way of teaching was through parables. This was because His intention was to be subversive – to overturn people's lives. As they listened to Jesus sharing parables they did not hear any mention of God and so there was no challenge to their own independence. Their defences were relaxed and this allowed His words to enter their hearts. Often they walked away perplexed, wondering what it was all about. But without them realising it, the parables lodged in their imagination. And then, perhaps weeks, months or even years later, the truth would explode like a time bomb in their unprotected hearts. They would realise that even though Jesus had not specifically mentioned God and the things of the kingdom, this was really what He had been talking about. Those whose hearts were soft towards God no doubt gave themselves deeply to Him, whereas those who resisted His words were being warned that if they persisted in their hard-hearted defiance they were heading for spiritual personal disaster.

Some might regard this as a kind of invasion, but that is not so. 'God's truth is not an alien invasion,' says Eugene Peterson, 'but a loving courtship in which the details of our common lives are treated as seeds in our conception, growth and maturity in the kingdom. Parables trust our imaginations, which is to say, our faith.' Human integrity is preserved because the truth does not overpower the will but rather seeks to overcome it by entreaty and persuasion. If you are a disciple of Jesus, you became one – not because you were overpowered but because you were loved. You are the object of a friendly invasion.

FURTHER STUDY

Amos 7:1–13;
Mark 12:1–12;
1 Pet. 2:7–10

1. What reaction did Amos' stories produce?
2. What reaction resulted from Jesus' parable?

Yes, heavenly Father, yes. I am so grateful for this 'friendly invasion' that brought my soul into living fellowship with You. In You, my Father, I have found everything my heart ever longed for – and more. Amen.

A bigger vision of Jesus

FOR READING & MEDITATION – MATTHEW 8:23–27

'He replied, "You of little faith, why are you so afraid?"' (v26)

As we continue to look at what we can learn from Jesus about our calling, we come to one of the most important matters for a disciple of Jesus – the nature of faith.

While Jesus and His disciples were crossing from one side of the Sea of Galilee to the other, a fierce storm came down on the lake causing the disciples to fear for their lives. Matthew, Mark and Luke each tell the story from their own perspective but all three make it clear that there was great fear in the hearts of every one of the disciples that day. There was not just one storm on Galilee but thirteen – one on the lake and twelve in the hearts of the disciples! Jesus, however, was asleep and apparently unperturbed by what was happening. When He is awakened by the frantic and fearful disciples, His first response is to challenge their 'little faith' and question why they are so afraid. 'Little faith' is what we demonstrate when we are just hanging on by our fingertips. That kind of faith is easily swamped by the waves of doubt and fear.

The degree of our faith is measured by our understanding of the stature of the One in whom we believe. Years ago, J.B. Phillips wrote a book entitled *Your God is Too Small*. It highlights that you will never rise higher in your Christian life than your concept of God. If you have a small concept of God, then your faith will be correspondingly small. The twelve disciples on the lake that day were about to discover the stature of the One they were following. As He rose and commanded the waves to be still, they gained a far bigger vision of His greatness and power. The treatment for 'little faith' is always a bigger vision of Jesus.

FURTHER STUDY

Mark 9:2–10;
2 Tim. 1:7–12;
2 Pet. 1:16–21

1. What gave Peter a bigger vision of Jesus?

2. What vision of Jesus did Paul remind Timothy of?

Heavenly Father, I see that to grow in faith is not to try to boost my faith through self-effort but to gain a bigger vision of Jesus. Open my eyes, I pray, so that I see even more clearly the majesty of Your beloved Son. Amen.

He cares

FOR READING & MEDITATION – MARK 4:35–41

'He said to his disciples, "Why are you so afraid? Do you still have no faith?"' (v40)

As we look at another account of the storm on the lake, we notice that Mark places a different emphasis on the conversation between Jesus and His disciples. Whereas Matthew has Jesus saying 'You of little faith,' Mark reports Him as saying, 'Do you still have no faith?' Jesus challenges the disciples, saying that they responded with not just 'little faith' but 'no faith'. Rather, they had panicked at the situation. They could not see that He slept so peacefully in the midst of the storm because He trusted implicitly in the Father's sovereignty and care.

The disciples, it seems, misinterpreted Jesus' sleep as indifference to their fate. 'Don't you care if we drown?' (v38). 'Don't you care?' I wonder how they reached the point where they believed Jesus did not care about them. This surely is the saddest unbelief of all. To doubt Jesus' power is one thing, but to doubt that He cares is the worst character assassination of all. Some of you will be aware of Rabbi Kushner, who wrote the bestseller *When Bad Things Happen to Good People* – interesting but it is off-beam biblically. Kushner doubted that God has the power to change things, but at least he did not doubt that God cares.

FURTHER STUDY

Eph. 2:3–13;
Titus 3:3–8

1. How does God demonstrate His love for us?

2. What saying is worthy of our trust?

The disciples were the men who had been sharing their lives with Jesus, had been taught by Him and cared for by Him; but now they were overcome by what they saw around them rather than trusting in Jesus Himself. It has often been said that we should not let go of in the dark that which we discovered in the light. From time to time doubts may arise in our hearts, but let us not doubt the truth that Jesus cares. He has done too much for us to ever entertain that groundless idea.

Lord Jesus, if ever a doubt about Your love and care for me arises in my heart, please help me to see it immediately. You have done so much for me. Let me not allow such a doubt to linger in my mind, let alone take possession of it. Amen.

Always in control

FOR READING & MEDITATION – MARK 4:35–41

'Jesus was in the stern, sleeping on a cushion.' (v38)

We spend another day looking at Mark's account of the stilling of the storm, this time to pick up on his statement, 'Jesus was in the stern, sleeping on a cushion.' Sailors say that the worst possible place to be in a storm is the stern of a boat. Yet here was Jesus in the worst possible place, enjoying what must have been the best possible peace.

What a lesson that was for the panic-stricken disciples. Confidence in His Father's love and care of Him allowed Jesus to sleep and let His Father deal with the storm. This is not to be taken to mean that when we find ourselves in a storm we close our eyes in denial and hope everything will be all right. If there is something that needs to be done, then we pay attention to it. As people sometimes say: God helps those who help themselves. In this situation, however, the disciples could do nothing to help themselves; they were entirely at the mercy of the storm. What they learnt was that when you have done all that you can and there is still no change, you continue to trust God to bring you safely through.

FURTHER STUDY

Rom. 5:6–11;
1 John 2:28–3:3;
3:21–24

1. What confidence did Paul have in God's love?

2. How did John encourage his readers to have confidence?

A story is told of a man by the name of John Bentley who was prone to worry. One night as he struggled to get to sleep, troubled by something that he could not deal with using his own wit and wisdom, he thought he heard the Lord say to him, 'John, why don't you go to sleep and I will stay up and do the worrying?' Well, we can question whether God really did say that to him, and we certainly know God does not worry, but let's not miss the point: if there is something to worry about, we turn the matter over to God. He worries over nothing because He is able to handle everything.

Heavenly Father, when I have done everything I need to do, please help me to relax and rest in the sure knowledge that You are in charge. Help me to trust You all the way. In Jesus' name. Amen.

If only...

Already we have looked at one incident – the storm on the lake – through two different pairs of eyes. Today we take another look at the same incident – this time through the eyes of Luke. We do so because we shall discover another aspect of faith that every disciple of Jesus ought to understand.

Luke's understanding of the situation is that after He was awakened Jesus asked His disciples, 'Where is your faith?' For Luke, the concern in the heart of the Master was not so much that they had no faith but that the faith they had was not being put to use. Frequently there is talk about having a mid-life crisis; here the disciples were in a mid-lake crisis. And when they needed their faith most, they could not find it. We should be careful not to criticise the disciples too enthusiastically, for if we were to look into our own hearts we might realise that we too have a tendency to mislay our faith. It is so easy to feel full of faith in a Sunday worship service, but when we hit a mid-week crisis we wonder where the faith we had on Sunday has gone.

The way to develop and sustain faith is to listen attentively to what Jesus says to us. The disciples had heard Jesus say, 'Let's go over to the other side' (v22), but for some reason they overlooked or forgot what He had said. They should have known that if Jesus said, 'We're going over to the other side of the lake,' then that is where they would finish up. The storm could not possibly sink the boat in which Jesus was sailing. The disciples couldn't go under because they were going over. If only they had remembered that Jesus is true to His word. If only...

FURTHER STUDY

Acts 13:42–52;
Heb. 12:1–3

1. How did God's Word spread in a time of crisis?

2. On whom should we fix our eyes so as not to lose heart?

Father, help me to learn this lesson also – that You always keep Your word. Not one of Your promises has ever been broken. I rest my faith and confidence on that glorious fact. Amen.

A stretched faith

FOR READING & MEDITATION – MARK 6:35–44

'"How many loaves do you have?" he asked. "Go and see."' (v38)

O n almost every page of the Gospels we see Jesus putting His disciples into situations which stretched their faith and understanding to the very utmost. Before we look at the details of the remarkable story we have read today let's pause and reflect on the fact that the miracle of the feeding of the five thousand mirrors the provision of manna in the wilderness at the beginning of Israel's history. The message reconfirms that in Jesus, Israel's God is bringing about a new and greater exodus.

FURTHER STUDY

Luke 24:13–27;
John 20:24–31

1. What happened to the disciples who were slow on the uptake?

2. Why did John write his Gospel?

There are many who wonder why, since Jesus could feed five thousand, He does not end the world's hunger at one stroke. Miracles like this took place not as acts of arbitrary power but as signs of the presence of God's kingdom in Jesus. Most probably the disciples had a hard time coming to terms with this. Everything that happened was outside their previous experience, and so we can forgive them for being slow on the uptake.

First of all, they were understandably concerned about the practicalities of the situation: 'It's late,' they said. 'Send the hungry crowd home to eat.' 'You give them something to eat,' Jesus told them. 'It would cost eight months' wages to pay for that,' was their hasty reply. Somewhere in the crowd they managed to find five loaves and two fish and watched while Jesus offered these up and the miraculous multiplication took place.

The life of discipleship is often like that. We come on the scene with our limited understanding and then try to convince Jesus with our arguments about how impracticable and impossible things are. Then we stand amazed as He takes what we give Him and works the most astonishing miracles. Amazing!

Lord Jesus, forgive us that we are so slow to understand, and even remonstrate with You. Increase our faith, dear Lord, we pray. For Your own name's sake. Amen.

Afraid – of Him?

FOR READING & MEDITATION – JOHN 6:16–24

'But he said to them, "It is I; don't be afraid."' (v20)

Here again the disciples were out of their depth in a boat on the Sea of Galilee. As it got dark, a strong wind started to blow, with the result that they found themselves toiling and rowing but getting nowhere. Then Jesus came to them, walking on the water. They were afraid, thinking He was a ghost (see Matt. 14:26). But as He spoke to them they let Him into their boat and, reassured by His presence, they immediately reached their destination.

Is that not typical of the life of discipleship? So often we strive for what seem unreachable goals, and what we do seems to end in futility. We toil in rowing, 'up against it', and get nowhere. Then Jesus comes and what happens? We are afraid of Him; He is not like us and seems at home in the impossible. This is our first reaction. Then eventually we let Him in and before we know it, we are at the place we intended to go. We read that when Jesus first came to this world 'King Herod... was disturbed, and all Jerusalem with him' (Matt. 2:3). He was disturbed at the coming of the Deliverer!

E. Stanley Jones said concerning this fear expressed by Herod and others in Jerusalem that 'they were naturalised in their lost-ness'. The disciples, too, sensed they were caught up in something bigger, and because they couldn't understand it they were afraid of it.

Should we be afraid of Jesus when He comes to us in ways that are beyond our understanding? Should the flower be afraid of the coming of the sunshine? Should the heart be afraid at the coming of love? We will never fully understand Jesus. It's best to accept whatever He does as always being the right thing at the right time.

FURTHER STUDY

Acts 10:9–10;
Rev. 1:9–18

1. How was Peter reconciled to something beyond his understanding?

2. How was John reassured when faced with the supernatural?

Gracious and loving Lord, may I never keep You at a distance because of fear or misunderstanding. Make me as comfortable with the supernatural as You are. For Your own dear name's sake. Amen.

'Mountaintop intercession'

FOR READING & MEDITATION – MARK 6:45–52

'After leaving them, he went up on a mountainside to pray.' (v46)

W e continue considering the story of the miraculous appearance of Jesus to His disciples during a storm on Galilee. Mark draws our attention to something very significant: after the disciples set out in the boat, Jesus went up onto a mountain to pray. Mark tells us also that when the boat was in the middle of the lake, Jesus was alone on the land (v47). Presumably, from His vantage point on the mountain, Jesus could see the disciples toiling in rowing and He might well have still been watching their progress as the darkness closed in on them.

FURTHER STUDY

Luke 22:31–32;
John 17:20–26;
Rom. 8:32–39;
Heb. 7:23–25

1. What did Jesus pray for Simon Peter?

2. What did Jesus pray for us?

What thoughts were in the mind of the Saviour at that moment? What was He praying about during His time alone with His heavenly Father? We can only speculate, but did He, during His prayer time, realise that the wind was getting up, become aware of His disciples' problems and arrive at a plan to come to their aid through a miracle? Did He see this as another opportunity to reveal something more of Himself to His disciples?

It has been suggested that, for us, the most significant part of this story is not so much the miracle on the water but Jesus' prayer time on the mountainside, for following that prayer time came an incident that gave the disciples a new revelation of His majesty and His love. Every one called by Jesus can rest in the knowledge that as we venture out on the lake of life He is watching over us and is engaged in mountaintop intercession. In our Christian life the greatest thing is not our own prayer life – vital as that is – but the fact that Jesus prays for us (see Heb. 7:25). In the end, our deepest comfort is not that God answers our prayers but that God answers His.

Dear Saviour, what comfort and peace it gives me to know that You are watching over me and praying for me through every hour of every day. Your intercession is my heart's consolation. Thank You dear Master. Amen.

Get out of the boat

*'But when he saw the wind, he was afraid and, beginning to sink,
cried out, "Lord, save me!"' (v30)*

We reflect further on the incident we have been looking at over the past two days – the miraculous appearance of Jesus as He walked on the Sea of Galilee. Matthew adds an important detail to the narrative also told by John and Mark. From him we learn that when the disciples see Jesus walking on the water, Peter – no surprise here – boldly urges Jesus to invite him to do the same! 'Come on, then', Jesus replies. The rest, as we say, is history. Peter walked on the water for a while, but when he looked down and saw the waves beneath his feet, he lost his nerve and began to sink. When he called out, 'Lord, save me!' Jesus didn't hesitate. He reached out, grabbed his hand and said, 'Faint-heart, what got into you?' (*The Message*). Simon Peter was saved from drowning by the gracious intervention of Jesus.

Let's not forget, though, that the central focus of this story, quite rightly, is Jesus Himself. Everything that happened was intended to reveal to the disciples new aspects of Jesus' personality and to show to them that He was who He said He was – God in human form. Thankfully they grasped some of the truth that Jesus intended them to learn for we read: 'Then those who were in the boat worshipped him, saying, "Truly you are the Son of God"' (v33).

We can all learn that Jesus responds positively to those who answer His call and venture forth boldly for the sake of the kingdom. It's worth remembering too that before Simon Peter started to sink he actually did walk on water. The waves became like a pavement beneath his feet. Perhaps there's a lesson here that we ought not to miss: if we want to walk on water then we have to get out of the boat.

FURTHER STUDY

Luke 11:5–13;
Acts 4:23–31

1. What does Jesus teach on praying with boldness?

2. How did God answer the believers' prayer?

Gracious Lord, can it be that there are things not happening in my life because I am afraid to step out? Though I know You don't want me to take reckless risks, perhaps I need to be bolder. Please help me dear Saviour. Amen.

Do you believe in miracles?

FOR READING & MEDITATION – MARK 6:45–56

*'Then he climbed into the boat with them, and the wind died down.
They were completely amazed' (v51)*

For one more day we consider the moments when Jesus appeared to His disciples walking on the water. The verse chosen as our text tells us that the disciples were amazed at what they had witnessed; they just could not understand what was going on. Eugene Peterson paraphrases part of today's reading in this way: 'They didn't understand what he had done at the supper. None of this had yet penetrated their hearts' (*The Message*).

It says a great deal for the integrity of the Gospel writers that they so endearingly and honestly record their own flaws and failures. The fact that they did not understand what Jesus had done at the feeding of the five thousand suggests they had not yet fully grasped the Saviour's mission, hence their further confusion at Jesus walking on the water and His calming of the waves. We read 'their hearts were hardened' (v52), and at that moment they were no different from some of His outright opponents (see Mark 3:5). Scepticism and rationalism still seemed to play a strong part in the disciples' thinking even though they had witnessed some most amazing events.

There are many in today's Church who struggle over the issue of miracles. The belief in miracles seems to me to be an important part of being a disciple of Jesus. C.S. Lewis put it this way: 'The mind which asks for a non-miraculous Christianity is a mind in process of relapsing from Christianity into mere "religion".' Why are we reluctant to believe in miracles? Conversion itself is a miracle. And when we become Christians we experience one miracle after another. The power of Jesus exceeded the rational abilities of His disciples. It always does.

FURTHER STUDY

1 Cor. 1:18–25;
Heb. 3:12–14

1. What does Paul tell us about man's wisdom?

2. What does the writer to Hebrews warn us about?

Lord Jesus Christ, forgive us if our hearts are so hardened by rationalism and scepticism that we cannot see that which is beyond the scope of our natural minds. Help us dear Saviour. Amen.

So many ways to experience
the Bible every day

There is nothing more life-changing and affirming than making time for daily Bible reading and engagement with God. At CWR, we believe this wholeheartedly.

We create Bible reading resources to help people discover how accessible and relevant God's Word is today. Perhaps you know someone who would benefit from one our devotional books or daily Bible reading notes (like *Every Day with Jesus*)? We have resources for every age, and for different stages or aspects of the Christian life. There is much to explore!

www.cwr.org.uk

With Steve and Bekah Legg, we have created *All Together: The Family Devotional*, which will be available this March. It speaks to all ages and explores Bible stories, biblical truths and key characters, helping readers to draw closer to God, and each other, through His Word.

To find out more, visit
www.cwr.org.uk/familydevotional

A class by Himself

FOR READING & MEDITATION – MARK 8:27–30

'"But what about you?" he asked. "Who do you say I am?"' (v29)

Now we start to think about another situation in which we find Jesus teaching His disciples the meaning of discipleship. In today's passage Jesus is seen with His disciples near the cool and pleasant town of Caesarea Philippi, which was on the northern boundary of Israel. In effect, He took them on a 'retreat'. Drawing the disciples aside from the hustle and bustle of the crowds attracted by His ministry, Jesus asks them what people were saying about Him. They report the popular rumours sweeping through Galilee that a remarkable prophet had arisen or even been reincarnated.

FURTHER STUDY

Acts 2:22–24, 32–41; 10:36–43

1. In what ways is Jesus more than a prophet?

2. In what terms does Peter preach this to Cornelius?

It was not surprising that people had reached these conclusions. In some ways Jesus behaved like the prophets of Israel's history. What is more, His message, like theirs, was a double-edged sword of both justice and grace. And there can be no doubt that He Himself had a keen sense of following in the prophetic tradition, which He revealed when He began to anticipate the fate that awaited Him in Jerusalem (see Luke 13:33). There were many people then, as now, who were prepared to recognise Jesus as a prophet but who were unable to see that He was more than a prophet.

It's interesting that this matter was raised by Jesus in the vicinity of Caesarea Philippi, for history records that the town had been recently renamed in honour of the Roman emperor and the local ruler, Philip, brother of Herod Antipas. Its original name was Paneas because it hosted a shrine to the Greek god Pan. Does Jesus fit into a pantheon of gods? The disciples needed to learn, as does the whole world, that Jesus doesn't belong in a class alongside others. He belongs in a class all by Himself.

Lord Jesus Christ, when will the world wake up to the truth that You are more than a prophet? You are the eternal Son of God – true God of true God. I am so grateful that my eyes have been opened to that great and glorious truth. Amen.

'Watch this space!'

FOR READING & MEDITATION – MATTHEW 16:13–20

*'Then he warned his disciples not to tell anyone
that he was the Christ.' (v20)*

Today we look at Matthew's account of what happened near Caesarea Philippi. When Jesus talked with His disciples to discover their true thoughts about Him, Simon Peter, the most outspoken disciple in the group, blurted out, 'You are the Christ, the Son of the living God' (v16). The Holy Spirit brought from the Father's heart to Peter's heart the revelation of who Jesus really is.

The Saviour then went on to talk about the crucial and foundational role that Peter's confession would have in the Church. We need have no fear about acknowledging that Peter was a founding apostle of the Church, since Peter's great sermon on the Day of Pentecost undoubtedly demonstrates this to be the case. What we are talking about here has nothing to do with tracing papal lineage back to Peter. Every true Christian church remains faithful to the confession given by Peter that day: Jesus is the Christ, the Son of the living God. It is important to note that this revelation, and not Peter's personality, was the rock on which Christ said He would build His Church.

Jesus cautioned His disciples about telling others who He was because at that point in His ministry it would have been easy for the crowds to get a totally wrong idea of His role as the Messiah. His many miracles might have led them to think of Him as nothing more than a divine miracle worker. In order to get a clear picture of His mission they needed to wait until after His death and resurrection. Jesus was saying in effect: 'Watch this space! In due time you will come to see the fullness of my mission here on earth. Then you will be able to tell the world who I really am.'

FURTHER STUDY

Acts 3:11–16, 18–26; 4:8–14; Rom. 4:16–25

1. How does Peter give his listeners the fuller picture?

2. How does Paul preach the same gospel as Peter?

Lord Jesus, how wonderful that we can now tell people who You really are. Forgive us when we are so slow to make known the good news that You are the Christ, the Son of God, the Saviour of the world. Forgive us and restore us. Amen.

Whose voice?

FOR READING & MEDITATION – MATTHEW 16:21–23

'Peter took him aside and began to rebuke him. "Never, Lord!" he said. "This shall never happen to you!"' (v22)

We are staying with the passage recording Peter's confession and Jesus' first prediction of His death in order to draw from it some further insights that will help us understand this roller coaster ride called discipleship. How amazing that the disciple who had just been commended for receiving the unique revelation from the Father was now being told he was doing the devil's work! With one ear he had listened to the voice of the Father in heaven; with the other he had listened to the voice of the devil.

FURTHER STUDY

Rom. 6:8–12; 1 Pet. 4:12–19

1. What does discipleship require according to Paul?

2. What does Peter say should be our attitude to suffering?

Without doubt, a wrong and misleading thought had been planted in Peter's mind when he tried to dissuade Christ from talking about going to a cross. This caused Jesus to say to Peter, 'Get behind me, Satan… you do not have in mind the things of God, but the things of men' (v23). The devil would have used everything in his power to keep Christ from the cross because he knew that Jesus' death there would bring his ultimate defeat. But there was no other way Christ could establish the kingdom of God without the suffering of the cross.

Our own battles with whose voice we listen to sometimes leads to suffering also. We do people a disservice when we misrepresent the gospel and deceive potential disciples into thinking that the Christian life is all a bed of roses. Regrettably, there are some churches which write the cost of discipleship in small print in the hope that it will escape people's attention. An example of this is a growing church that has dropped the 'repentance' session on the Alpha course because it might be too off-putting for today's seekers. Our repentance is where our transformation begins!.

Gracious and loving Lord, one truth seems to be coming at me from all directions: true discipleship requires not just a part of me but all. Help us as Your Church not to water down the gospel. For Your name's sake. Amen.

The divine 'must'

FOR READING & MEDITATION – MATTHEW 16:24–28

*'Then Jesus said to his disciples, "If anyone would come after me,
he must deny himself"' (v24)*

For one more day we consider this passage in which Jesus predicts His death and laid down in strong language what He asks of His followers. The 'must' of divine necessity which motivated Jesus also motivates those who become His disciples. We are to bear the yoke of discipleship in the same way that He bore the cross upon His shoulders. There is a 'must' in the heart of a disciple, just as there was in the heart of the Saviour. We must deny ourselves, we are told, take up our cross and follow Him. But what does it mean to 'deny' oneself?

Let's try to clear a few things up for there are many strange and misguided ideas about the subject of self-denial. It involves much more than giving up chocolate or desserts for Lent! Some have even taken Jesus' instruction to mean that we must hate ourselves. True self-denial, however, has nothing to do with self-hatred or self-denigration. Rather, in this case it is the bold and courageous act of fully giving over our lives to Jesus and letting Him lead us. In other words, we surrender our lives into His hands and allow Him to shape and determine our destiny – not just for Lent but for the whole of our lifetime.

FURTHER STUDY

Rom. 12:1–3, 9–19;
Heb. 10:32–39;
13:20–21

1. What kind of lifestyle is pleasing to God?

2. What confidence does the writer of Hebrews want his readers to have?

Those who hesitate at what Jesus said need to consider carefully His words: 'What good will it be for a man if he gains the whole world, yet forfeits his soul?' (v26). What is the alternative to rejecting the claims and appeal of Jesus? It is the loss of one's soul. In the words of Jim Elliot, the missionary who was martyred by the Aucas of South America: 'That man is no fool who gives up what he cannot keep to gain what he cannot lose.'

Lord Jesus, may the same 'must' – the same energy and love that drove and motivated You – govern my life also. Help me be consumed with You to follow your call, to work for You and to honour You in every part of my life. In Your name I ask it. Amen.

'Take up the cross'

FOR READING & MEDITATION – MARK 8:34–37

'If anyone would come after me, he must deny himself and take up his cross and follow me.' (v34)

On different occasions, when explaining what it meant to answer the call of discipleship, Jesus openly said that they would have to 'take up the cross'. Just as people have misunderstood the command 'deny yourself', so too has this instruction been misconstrued.

In the days of Jesus, the phrase 'to carry the cross' had a quite specific and significant meaning. Under the ruthless rule of the occupying Romans, you would often have seen the frightening spectacle of a procession of people dragging their heavy cross-beams to the place of execution. And crucifixion – which was considered to be the most agonising and humiliating death – was reserved exclusively for revolutionaries and those convicted of crimes of violence. In other words, taking up the cross for the men and women of Jesus' day could mean quite literally having to give their lives for His cause.

As followers of Jesus, we can certainly expect to face public hostility and social discomfort as a result of answering His call to discipleship. To be clear, the 'cross' we are asked to carry is not a difficult boss or a cantankerous mother-in-law! To carry our cross is to lay down self-will and pick up God's will, and where the two collide we choose His will over our own. In some parts of the world, even as you read these lines somebody will be facing imprisonment torture and perhaps death for Jesus' sake. At present, those of us who live in the Western world mostly do not have to face that possibility, but what would happen if we did? Would we put Jesus first, even though our own lives were threatened by our doing so? It is without doubt the most challenging question we can ever be asked.

FURTHER STUDY

Phil. 1:19–26;
2 Tim. 4:6–8;
Rev. 12:10–12

1. How did Paul face the possibility of death?

2. How do Christians overcome the accuser?

Lord Jesus, it is so easy to answer 'Yes' if I know I am not likely to be in that position, but I pray with all my heart that my love for You will be greater than the love I have for myself or even the love I have for life. Help me dear Saviour. Amen.

'My way'

FOR READING & MEDITATION – LUKE 9:23–27

'For whoever wants to save his life will lose it, but whoever loses his life for me will save it.' (v24)

An aspect of discipleship we have yet to consider is Jesus' challenge to us to lose our lives in order to find them. In *The Message*, Eugene Peterson paraphrases Jesus' words here like this: 'Self-sacrifice is the way, *my* way, to finding yourself, your true self.' Notice the words '*my* way'. Jesus did not hesitate to put aside His own interests and He looks for the same in His disciples. We can be sure that He will never ask us to do what He was not prepared to do Himself.

By His baptism and during the wilderness temptations Jesus led by example in setting aside His own comfort to do His Father's will. In baptism He identified with sinners – and just in case anyone who saw Him entering the waters might have thought He was a sinner, God opened the heavens and said, 'This is my Son, whom I love; with him I am well pleased' (Matt. 3:17). In the temptations He refused to satisfy His hunger by using His name to turn the stones into bread, declined to make a spectacle of Himself to win a following, and turned down the offer of the kingdoms of this world on easy terms (see Matt. 4:1–11). He exemplified self-sacrifice all the way.

But what did Jesus mean when He said that if we lose ourselves we will find ourselves? People are desperately trying to find themselves – through work, money, entertainment, sport, relationships, and so on. But do they find themselves? Mostly, they find a fictional self, not the real self – the self made to glorify God and enjoy Him forever. No one can find their true self until they lose it for the sake of Christ and His kingdom. And having lost it, they find a self with which they can live, as we say, happily ever after.

FURTHER STUDY

Gal. 5:19–26;
1 John 3:16–20;
4:7–16

1. What characterises those who belong to Christ?

2. Of what level of self-sacrifice does John speak?

Lord Jesus, I do not want to live with a fictional self; I want to live with my real self, the self You want me to be – my true self. Lead me deeper into an understanding of this I pray. In Your name I ask it. Amen.

The 'how-much-more' God

FOR READING & MEDITATION – LUKE 12:22–34

'Therefore I tell you, do not worry about your life, what you will eat; or about your body, what you will wear.' (v22)

Jesus' instructions to His disciples here are ones that we, His twenty-first-century disciples, need to take to heart. 'Don't fuss about what's on the table at mealtimes,' He tells them, 'or if the clothes in your closet are in fashion' (v22, *The Message*). Of course, it is one thing to accept that we shouldn't fuss; it is another thing to practise it. So how do we break free from the habit of worrying over everything?

One way is by learning about the 'how-much-more' God (see v28). If God can take care of the ravens and the lilies and provide for them, how much more is He committed to His disciples. He calls us on this basis – the fact that we mean more to Him than birds or flowers – to trust Him. Our Father knows what we need.

FURTHER STUDY

Rom. 15:13;
Heb. 13:5–8;
1 Pet. 5:7–11

1. Meditate on Paul's prayer.

2. Why should we be content with what we have?

How often have you been in difficulty, wondering how you would fare, when suddenly something happened and the need was met? If we had more confidence in our Father's ability to intervene at every stage of our lives, we would spend less time worrying and more time praising. Living each day with resilience and a deep trust in the Father to provide for our needs is a powerful, if unglamorous, testimony to all who are seeking God. *The Message* puts it like this: 'People who don't know God and the way he works fuss over these things, but you know both God and how he works. Steep yourself in God-reality, God-initiative, God-provisions. You'll find all your everyday human concerns will be met' (v30).

Are any concerns troubling you at this moment? Trust God. Don't worry – He will meet with you in your need. He may keep you waiting until the last moment but as the old saying goes: there are trains on His line until 11.59!

Lord Jesus, You are speaking to me again. You know my tendency to worry over so many things. Forgive me, I pray, and give me an ever-growing consciousness of Your ability to take care of everything. Amen.

Lessons from a little child

FOR READING & MEDITATION – MARK 9:30–37

'Jesus called the Twelve and said, "If anyone wants to be first, he must be the very last, and the servant of all."' (v35)

Once again Jesus highlighted for His disciples the upside-down nature of life in God's kingdom, as He taught them an important lesson about status and power. Isn't it astonishing that while He was conscious of having to suffer and die for their sakes they were arguing about which of them was the greatest? When He asked them what they are arguing about, there was an embarrassed silence!

Of course, it's all too easy to criticise the disciples, but how often are we, too, caught out in our pride and competitiveness and power struggles, even as we profess to be following a Master who humbled Himself to serve? Like them, how slow we are to learn that the first shall be last and the servant of all. As He did so often, Jesus surprised the disciples with a timely object lesson. He took a child and stood him in their midst. Many people are puzzled by Jesus' action here, as children are seldom humble or angelic – except when they're asleep! Jesus, however, was not alluding to their behaviour; He is illustrating that a child is someone with a humble status who was absolutely dependent. In infancy a child depends on his parents for everything – bring me, fetch me, feed me, and so on. I believe it is John Stott who said, 'Children are rightly called "dependants"; for what they know they depend on what they have been taught, and for what they have they depend on what they have been given.'

Humility and dependence are to be the pre-eminent characteristics of those who are followers of Jesus Christ. If these are absent in those who call themselves disciples then they have not fully understood the nature of His call. They may carry the name but not the nature.

FURTHER STUDY

1 Cor. 9:19–23;
Gal. 5:13–14;
1 Pet. 2:11–17;
5:1–6

1. In what ways did Paul serve others?

2. How does Peter encourage both service and humility?

Lord Jesus, help me examine my heart in these moments to see whether or not these characteristics of humility and dependence are part of my personality. I long to be a disciple, not just in name but in nature also. In Your name I ask it. Amen.

What a Leader!

FOR READING & MEDITATION – MARK 10:32–34

*'They were on their way up to Jerusalem... and the disciples were
astonished, while those who followed were afraid.' (v32)*

Many have wondered what it must have been like to walk
and talk with Jesus. Many years ago, the singer Johnny
Cash fronted a film of the life of Jesus called *Gospel Road*. One
scene that grabbed the attention of viewers was a shot taken
from a high angle looking down on the 'disciples' as they
wandered along a lane together. It showed a bunch of young
men good-naturedly joking and laughing and jostling each other.
At one point the group even tried to throw 'Simon Peter' over a
wall! The film gave a vivid impression of the sheer humanness
of life among the disciples. Here, however, in the
passage before us now, there is no hilarity, no laughing
or pushing – for those who are travelling with Jesus
are aware He is on the road that will lead to His death.

**FURTHER
STUDY**

John 11:55–57;
12:12–15,
20–28

1. How did
Jesus face what
lay ahead?

2. How did
people respond
to His arrival?

We read that the disciples were 'astonished' and
others who followed were 'afraid'. Probably those
who followed and were afraid were pilgrims on their
way to the Passover in Jerusalem who had heard
that Jesus was going there to die. It is interesting
and at the same time impressive to watch how Jesus
handles the situation. Knowing what lies ahead of
Him, He does not draw back, but strides ahead of
them, leading the way.

What a graphic image this is of the Saviour's determination
to be, as the writer to the Hebrews says of Him, 'the author
and perfecter of our faith' (Heb. 12:2). Over the past weeks we
have seen Him in so many different situations, but the more
we see of Him, the more astonished we are at His courage,
determination and self-giving love. He is the One who goes
ahead of us into the eye of the storm to bear the judgment that
really was meant for us. What a leader! What a Saviour!

**My Saviour and my God, give me the courage to face whatever lies
ahead no matter how threatening or unpleasant it may be, knowing
that nothing can ever happen that we cannot handle together.
In Your name I pray. Amen.**

What shows on your face?

FOR READING & MEDITATION – LUKE 9:51–53

'but the people there did not welcome him, because he was heading for Jerusalem.' (v53)

Every face, it is said, tells its own story. A blush, a furrow of pain, or the steady gaze that comes from inner peace – these things can reveal what is going on deep inside us. Luke tells us that as the time came for Jesus to face the cross, He resolutely set out for Jerusalem. The New King James Version puts it like this: 'When the time had come for Him to be received up... He steadfastly set His face to go to Jerusalem' (v51). As W.E. Sangster memorably once titled a sermon, 'His destination is on His face'. Although geographically Jesus moved in several different directions after this, His overriding purpose was always to go to Jerusalem, there to suffer and die for us.

FURTHER STUDY

Acts 6:8–15; 7:54–60; 2 Cor. 3:12–18; 4:5–6,13–18

1. What story did Stephen's face tell?

2. What should our faces reflect?

The disciples were annoyed because the Samaritans refused them hospitality but Jesus did not share their irritation. Little did they realise it but Jesus, far from being frustrated with the inhospitable Samaritans, was on His way to die for them. The closer Jesus got to the cross, the more His determination to do the will of God showed in His countenance. God's will for Him was to walk straight into the firestorm of judgment in order to take it upon Himself and spare the lives of not just the Samaritans but anyone who will answer His call.

Does your destination show on your face? You, amazingly, are not heading for a cross but a crown. But can people see as they look at you that you are, in the words of the old hymn, 'marching upward to Zion, beautiful, beautiful Zion'? Every day something registers on our faces – anxiety, surprise, concern, anger, frustration. How wonderful it would be if people saw in our countenance something of our eternal destination – 'the beautiful city of God'.

Jesus, may I be so consumed with You that this will be apparent in everything I say and do. Your determination to do the will of God showed on Your face. May my determination to do Your will be seen on my face also. Amen.

A thing most beautiful

FOR READING & MEDITATION – MATTHEW 26:6–13

*'Jesus said to them, "Why are you bothering this woman?
She has done a beautiful thing to me."' (v10)*

The account of the woman anointing Jesus' head with her most precious perfume has been described as the sweetest and most moving scene in the whole of the Gospels. She ministered to Jesus in more ways than she imagined, for He interpreted her action as an anointing for His burial, days before His crucifixion.

The disciples reacted badly to this outpouring of love, objecting to the waste, and arguing that funds were being diverted from the poor. They were technically right, but spiritually wrong. Jesus never once played down the need to care for the poor. In verse 11 He quotes from Deuteronomy 15:11 – a verse in which giving to the poor is strongly emphasised. What mattered to Jesus at that moment was not how correct she was in terms of Old Testament law but how passionate was her devotion. That's what He defended; that's what He called 'beautiful'. And that's the picture He has ensured is remembered for all time, and the one He holds out for all His disciples. Wherever and whenever the gospel is preached, Jesus said, the story of what this woman did will be told.

There are many other events Jesus could have selected to be retold again and again. So why did He choose this one? Because the issue that matters to Jesus, the one that He holds dear to His heart, the one that brings a smile to His lips or a tear to His eye, is not how much we know, but how much we love. I once read in a devotional: 'Maybe this is why, when Pharisees were fighting over theology [and, we may add, the interpretation of Old Testament laws], prostitutes were falling at the Saviour's feet and slipping into the kingdom of God on their tears.'

FURTHER STUDY

Luke 7:39–50;
23:50–24:3

1. What did Jesus say distinguished the sinful woman from the Pharisee?

2. What devotion was shown to Jesus after His death?

Precious Saviour, thank You for showing me that what You enjoy most about me is not how much I know, but how much I love. I love You Lord Jesus. Help me to love You even more. Amen.

Living the Dream

Dave Smith, Senior Pastor of
KingsGate Community Church,
introduces *Living the Dream*.

***Living the Dream* follows the story of Joseph (Exod. 37–50).
Tell us, why Joseph?**

This story is truly inspiring. It starts with a picture of a spoilt
17-year-old from a dysfunctional family who received a dramatic
dream of future greatness. Clearly unprepared to 'live the dream',
he underwent a 13-year period of testing and preparation. So it's
all about the power of receiving a 'dream' from the Lord, embracing
His preparation, and experiencing His favour and blessing.

What is 'the dream'?

Primarily, the dream is for you to have an eternal love-relationship
with God, to become His child, to be loved and to love Him for all
eternity. But there is more. God has a purpose for your life that is
unique to you, and He wants to reveal it to you. Joseph lived the
dream, and so can you and I.

**What lessons do you glean from Joseph and explore in
Living the Dream?**

Like Joseph, we all have lessons to learn, such as the importance
of forgiving others, using our God-given gifts and thriving even
when times seem tough. Whatever your age or whatever stage of
life you are in, my prayer is that the Lord will use this book to help
transform the rest of your life.

Living the Dream is available from March.
To purchase, you can use the order form
at the back of these notes, or visit
www.cwr.org.uk/store
ISBN: 978-1-78259-665-3

When the going got tough...

FOR READING & MEDITATION – MATTHEW 26:47–56

'Then all the disciples deserted him and fled.' (v56)

These words are some of the saddest in Scripture. What kind of disciples were these who deserted their Master in His hour of need? Had Jesus failed to detect the faithlessness in His friends? Or, was it the case that they had not really heeded His challenges that a true disciple should be ready to lay down their life for Him and the gospel. Most likely it was the latter. A Jewish rabbi once said: 'At the door of a gift shop there are many brothers and friends; at the door of a prison there are no brothers and friends.'

FURTHER STUDY

Gal. 1:1–10;
2 Tim. 1:13–18;
4:9–18

1. What does Paul reaffirm in the midst of desertion?

2. What sort of loyalty did Paul expect and receive?

Judas, we read, betrayed Jesus with a kiss, even though Jesus called him 'friend'. Simon Peter betrayed the Saviour differently, by drawing and using his sword (see John 18:10), fuelling the suspicion that the cause of Christ was based on violent revolution, which, of course, it was not. Jesus explicitly renounced violence as the way to bring in the kingdom. Nor would He reach out for a spectacular deliverance. There in the Garden of Gethsemane He surrendered the right to divine intervention to spare His suffering just as He had done earlier, during the temptations.

When the going got tough for that band of disciples, the tough got going – in the opposite direction. At that moment in the Garden of Gethsemane Jesus had as much trouble with His followers as He did with His enemies. Yet, despite the confusion of His disciples and arrest by His enemies, the Saviour submitted Himself to the Father's will, which had already been spelt out in the Scriptures (vv54–56). How amazing that He did this this for you and me. Had there been no cross there would have been no salvation. Imagine it – we would still be in our sins.

Jesus, You are so wonderful. Amongst the confusion, while You were experiencing desertion and disloyalty, You thought not of Yourself but of those You were set on saving. I am so glad that that included me. Amen.

FOR READING & MEDITATION – MARK 15:16–20

'Then they led him out to crucify him.' (v20)

We come once again to Good Friday, the day when we mark in a special way our Saviour's death on the cross. Although so far in this issue we have been thinking about the call and cost of discipleship, today we focus on what our salvation cost the Saviour. In simple terms, it meant that He took on Himself the punishment for sin which we ourselves should have borne. An illustration might help.

Many years ago in India, a young boy was adopted by a headmaster and his wife. The boy became increasingly wayward and rebellious. One day after the boy had committed a wilful act of disobedience, the headmaster took a cane and told the boy to hold out his hand. The boy stood there defiant and full of bravado but stretched out his hand. The headmaster brought down the cane heavy and hard... not on the boy's hand, but on his own. Seeing what had happened, the boy cried out with inner pain, fell at his father's feet and asked for forgiveness. After that the boy was completely different and later became a bishop in India. Every Good Friday he would tell that story to illustrate how his father's suffering broke something inside of him and freed him from himself.

FURTHER STUDY

1 Tim. 2:1–7;
1 John 2:1–6

1. For whom did Jesus give His life as a ransom?

2. For whose sins did Jesus atone?

Gaze once again on the cross. Appreciate afresh the central and most glorious truth of the Christian gospel, that God in the Person of Jesus bent to deal with mankind's predicament and on the cross paid the full penalty for our sin. The sins which nailed Him to the tree – prejudice, selfishness, blame-shifting, arrogance, and so on – are the same sins that we have committed. In that sense, it can be said of us that we also crucified the Son of God. Yes, we were there when they crucified our Lord.

Dear Saviour, I realise afresh that You were put to death not by one or two monstrously malicious sins but by an accumulation of ordinary sins – the sins I myself have committed. For that I am eternally grateful. Amen.

Man's worst – God's best

FOR READING & MEDITATION – JOHN 19:28–37

'Jesus said, "It is finished." With that, he bowed his head and gave up his spirit.' (v30)

In the interval between Good Friday and Easter Sunday we remain at the foot of the cross. The question is often asked by those who know something of the life of Christ: How can it be that a Being so true, so loving, so perfect, was done to death while still comparatively young? He was only in His early thirties when He died. Surely it borders on the incredible that the human race should treat Christ, the most perfect man who ever walked on this earth, in the way it did. Many regard His crucifixion as the greatest felony in history.

FURTHER STUDY

Isa. 53:3–11;
Heb. 9:11–15

1. What part did God play in the death of Jesus?

2. How did Jesus obtain redemption?

The truth is, of course, that this greatest of human crimes became the greatest of heaven's blessings. Jesus took upon Himself our sins and bore them all away. But people ask: couldn't God have forgiven our sin without sending His Son to a cross? Would God have allowed it had there been any other option? In a righteous universe there is always justice. Even our own blunted conscience has enough sharpness in it to tell us that. Sin is so contrary to God and to His holiness. It is so awful, so affronting that no human mind can grasp just how opposed it is to the nature of God. Only holiness can perceive holiness. There was only one way for God to overcome sin: He had to bear the punishment Himself. On that green hill outside the city wall (to use the words of an old hymn) God in the Person of His Son drew sin to battle – and won. Something was completed at Calvary which never needed to be repeated.

No human mind can fully comprehend how the price of sin was paid on the cross, but the fact that it was is the message of the whole New Testament. We may not be able to fully understand it but we most certainly can fully stand upon it.

Jesus, Son of God and Saviour of my soul, I am humbled by Your willingness to come to earth, die on a cross, all in order to save me. My soul has been won by You. I worship forever at Your feet – Your humble and obedient disciple. Amen.

The most glorious dawn

FOR READING & MEDITATION – MATTHEW 28:1–10

'at dawn on the first day of the week, Mary Magdalene and the other Mary went to look at the tomb.' (v1)

On this Easter Day our thoughts focus on the glorious resurrection of the Saviour. The women who loved Jesus and followed Him were anxious to offer their last expression of devotion to Him by anointing His body with spices. It is only a small ministry that can be exercised upon the body of a loved one who has died, but love always insists on offering it.

The Gospel writers tell us that the women hurried to the tomb just as dawn was breaking. There was no man in the party, as this kind of ministry was usually performed by women, and women alone. They knew the tomb was sealed with a great stone, and Mark says they murmured to one another as they walked there, 'Who will roll the stone away from the entrance of the tomb?' (Mark 16:3). But when they arrived they found that the stone has already been rolled away. A white-robed youth addressed them: 'There's nothing to fear here. I know you're looking for Jesus, the One they nailed on the cross. He is not here. He was raised, just as he said... Now, get on your way quickly' (vv6–7, *The Message*).

Some years ago, a programme on television entitled *The World's Most Glorious Dawn* dealt with the landing of the Allied Forces on the Normandy beaches, which led ultimately to the end of World War II. That, said the programme makers, was the most glorious dawn in history. I disagree. The most glorious dawn in history was when the Son of God stepped from His garden grave in the power of an endless life. The radiance of that dawn has spread its golden glow over the whole of history. There was never a dawn like it before and there will never be a dawn like it again. Christ lives!

FURTHER STUDY

Acts 13:26–37;
1 Cor. 15:12–25;
Col. 1:9–14

1. How important is Jesus' resurrection to Paul?

2. What kind of kingdom has Jesus brought us into?

Lord Jesus Christ, the radiance of that glorious dawn when You rose again from the dead lights up my soul. Because You live, I live also. And not just in time but also in eternity. I am so thankful. Amen.

The real thing

FOR READING & MEDITATION – LUKE 10:23–24

*'Then he turned to his disciples and said privately,
"Blessed are the eyes that see what you see."' (v23)*

We can only speculate as to how clear it was to the early disciples that they were some of the most privileged people on earth because they rubbed shoulders every day with Jesus Himself. The poet William Wordsworth recalled the naive excitement and optimism of those who welcomed the revolutionary movements in eighteenth-century Europe in these lines: 'Bliss was it in that dawn to be alive, and to be young was very heaven.' What bliss it must have been for the disciples to walk with Jesus day after day and be part of His revolutionary programme.

FURTHER STUDY

Acts 5:41–42;
Eph. 1:3–14;
1 Pet. 1:10–12

1. What privilege did the apostles rejoice in?

2. What are the privileges of salvation?

If the disciples did not realise how privileged they were, then they must have been really out of touch with the world around them. World history had reached the turning-point; they were living through God's saving revolution, the arrival of His kingdom. It was for this day that the kings and prophets had longed. Surely some of the disciples must have grasped the significance of what was happening, though sometimes when we look at their behaviour, we wonder.

Of course, living as we do in this day and age when the Spirit has come to illuminate our minds and hearts, we have the advantage over them. And we also have the true witness of these first disciples, written in hindsight after the resurrection, on which to base our faith. Living now, as we do, on this side of Easter, we are even more privileged. It would have been wonderful to have lived in the days of Jesus – the other side of Easter – but surely as Jesus Himself said to Thomas: 'Because you have seen me, you have believed; blessed are those who have not seen and yet have believed' (John 20:29). Do you realise how blessed you are?

Lord Jesus, I can never know just how privileged the disciples felt to be close to You but I know how privileged I feel to be called as one of Your disciples. Nothing that has ever happened or could happen can be more wonderful. Amen.

Little prayer – little power

FOR READING & MEDITATION – MARK 9:14–29

'He replied, "This kind can come out only by prayer."' (v29)

This ninth chapter of Mark's Gospel contains an amazing contrast. It begins with Christ's glorious transfiguration on the mountain top and then moves to the scene of confusion down in the valley. Mark describes vividly what we meet there: chaotic crowds, argumentative religious types, hand-wringing do-gooders, puzzled sceptics, muddled half-believers, out-of-control children and desperate parents. And there, too, we meet the disciples of Jesus who seem unable to make a difference. Three of the disciples had witnessed Jesus' transfiguration but the disciples appear powerless and paralysed.

How this mirrors, generally speaking, life in the Church today. No amount of subtle editing can disguise how the Church can on occasions seem paralysed by its own sense of helplessness, lack of understanding and prayerlessness. The reason why the disciples couldn't cast out the evil spirit, explained Jesus, was because they 'come out only by prayer'. He did not mean that they had not prayed enough immediately before attempting to exorcise the demon, but rather that any effective ministry must be underpinned by a lifestyle of prayer. Thankfully we are not alone in these situations, and like the father of the child we can say, 'I do believe; help me overcome my unbelief.' Our authority lies not in us alone but in the One who has called us – Jesus.

FURTHER STUDY

Eph. 6:10–20;
1 Thess. 5:16–28;
2 Thess. 1:11–12; 3:1–5

1. What must we do to be 'strong in the Lord'?
2. What is Paul's prayer for the Thessalonians?

We can begin to see from Jesus' statement why He spent so much time in prayer. In those times, He waited upon His Father for the spiritual strength He needed for whatever He wanted Him to do. That's the way it is with prayer. Little prayer, little power. A lot of prayer, a lot of power.

Heavenly Father, I understand that the more time I spend with You in prayer the more I perceive Your will. Forgive me if I am prone to rely on my own strength rather than Yours. Help me be willing to spend more time with You in prayer. Amen.

Prowess in prayer

FOR READING & MEDITATION – LUKE 11:1–13

'When he finished [praying], one of his disciples said to him,
"Lord, teach us to pray"' (v1)

Someone once defined a disciple as a person who has learned to pray the Lord's Prayer. They meant, of course, not just reciting the words but praying with a full understanding of it. However, to call this the 'Lord's Prayer' is really a misnomer as Jesus was not saying, 'This is how I pray,' but 'This is how you can pray.' Jesus would never pray, for example, 'Forgive us our sins,' for He had no sins to be forgiven although, of course, other aspects of the prayer we can well imagine Him praying.

It is interesting that although Jesus was the greatest teacher the world has ever known, the disciples never asked Him, 'Lord, teach us to preach'. But there was something about His prayer life that arrested their attention. What was it? Perhaps more than anything it was that it showed His total reliance on God His Father for daily strength and direction. They must have sensed it was this Father–Son relationship which sustained Jesus in everything. A quick overview of the life of Jesus, from His baptism to His suffering on the cross, reveals that at every step of the way He relied on the Father's presence and power being there for Him.

Examine the prayer closely and you will see that it breathes an atmosphere of dependence. It begins with recognising that God is our Father. Then follows an admission of dependence on Him for our daily bread and our protection against temptation. The person who defined a disciple as a person who has learned to pray the Lord's Prayer was in many ways right. Only prayerful trust in our heavenly Father will enable us to live the life of discipleship and sustain us in all we do.

FURTHER STUDY

John 5:16–23;
1 Cor. 15:27–28;
2 Cor. 1:8–11

1. How did Jesus describe His dependence on His Father?
2. In what circumstances did Paul learn the secret of dependence?

Lord Jesus, the more I learn about You the more I see that Your strength while here on earth was Your absolute dependence on Your Father. I long for that strength to be mine also. Please teach me to be a more dependent disciple. Amen.

The Father–Son relationship

FOR READING & MEDITATION – MATTHEW 6:5–15

*'This, then, is how you should pray: "Our Father in heaven,
hallowed be your name"' (v9)*

So important are the issues connected with what we call the
Lord's Prayer that we spend another day considering it. The
disciples had been nourished by the great uplifting prayers
of the prophets – Isaiah, Jeremiah, Ezekiel, and others – but
recognised that the prayer life of Jesus was in a league of its
own. They had never heard anyone pray like Jesus, hence their
request, 'Lord, teach us to pray' (Luke 11:1). As we explored
yesterday, the one thing above all others that would have
struck the disciples about the prayer life of Jesus was that it
revealed His absolute dependence on His Father for
everything. And it is this Father–Son relationship
that He wants also for us.

**FURTHER
STUDY**

Eph. 2:14–22;
3:7–13;
Heb. 2:10–13;
4:14–16; 5:7–9

We, of course, are not 'sons' in the same sense that
Jesus was God's Son, but in Christ we are sons and
daughters having the same rights of access to the
Father as He did. Following Jesus, then, is a life of
dependence on the Father's goodness in the service
of His kingdom and in obedience to His will. It may
involve us in forgoing many of the securities we have
come to rely on, which the world promises to provide.
In laying down this model of prayer for His disciples,
Jesus lovingly welcomes us into His own warm and
shatterproof fellowship with His Father.

1. What
attitudes did
Jesus express
in His own
prayer life?
2. How are we
to approach
God?

What a gift our Lord gave us when He framed this
prayer. One sentiment that has always spoken to me is: 'We
don't choose the prayer; it chooses us. It reaches out to us,
forms us, invites us into the adventure called discipleship.' But
it is not just a form of prayer; beneath lies a whole philosophy
about prayer. God save us from merely reciting it without
realising what underlies it.

**Lord Jesus, every time I recite the Lord's Prayer help me to
remember what lies beneath the words and teach me, I pray, to
have the same dependence on the Father that You so wonderfully
demonstrated. In Your name I ask it. Amen.**

Our family tree

FOR READING & MEDITATION – JOHN 19:17–27

'he said to his mother, "Dear woman, here is your son," and to the disciple, "Here is your mother."' (vv26–27)

In times of deep crisis it is a great comfort to be surrounded by those we love and those whom we know love us. Jesus, in His death, must have derived some comfort from seeing His mother and His closest disciple at the foot of the cross. Characteristically, He thought more of them than of Himself, and in His dying words provided for a relationship of mutual support and commitment for the remainder of their lives. Speaking to His mother, He said, 'Dear woman, here is your son,' and to the disciple, 'Here is your mother.'

FURTHER STUDY

Matt. 5:38–48;
Eph. 4:1–5,
14–16; 4:25–5:2

1. Why does Jesus ask us to love our enemies?

2. How does our love overflow for one another?

This bond, formed on the level ground at the foot of the cross, has characterised Christ's Church throughout the centuries. Commentators Richard Bauckham and Trevor Hart put it like this: 'Just as Jesus' mother and the Beloved Disciple would not otherwise have been related had not Jesus at His death brought them together and charged them with being mother and son to each other, so the Church is the community of people who would not otherwise be related, but whom the crucified Jesus brings together, forging new relationships through His death for us.' This is why we say that there are no strangers in the Body of Christ, just brothers and sisters we may not have met yet.

Because of Jesus' words Mary's burden of pain was shared, while John took on an important new ministry and calling. In the shadow of the cross John was bound to Mary and Mary to John in a new relationship. That same cross binds all those called disciples together in a way that is beyond anything natural. It is by Christ's love for us and His love flowing through us to one another that others may know we are His disciples. The cross is our family tree.

Lord Jesus, this truth challenges me deeply: that I am bound not only to You but to everyone else who is bound to You. May the love You have for me and the love I have for You overflow both to those who love You and those who don't. Amen.

Shock tactics

*'If anyone... does not hate his father and mother...
he cannot be my disciple.' (v26)*

Several times over the past few weeks we have seen how Jesus shocked His hearers with the most challenging statements. Many people think that the words found in today's reading are among the most shocking and sensational He had ever spoken. They certainly sound harsh and unloving. Unless we understand what Jesus was getting at when He spoke these words we can easily run away with the erroneous idea that He did not support family values.

Jesus was emphasising, once again, that our relationship with Him takes precedence over every other relationship. The words 'hate his father and mother', and so on, are not be taken to mean that disciples are to feel anger towards or detest their parents or any other of their relations, but rather that they are to put Jesus, His cause and His kingdom above and before everyone else to whom they relate.

Why does Jesus talk like this? Because He has come not to hold a party but a rescue mission – a rescue mission to save the world. The mission is so important that, like invasion troops before going into any major conflict or perilous mission, His followers may have to write their last letters home, set aside their own possessions and put their lives at risk. If we really understood the real emergency, He seems to be saying, brought on by the arrival of God's kingdom in our midst, we would be willing to go without our most precious things and rally to His cause. As Dallas Willard puts it, 'As long as one thinks anything is really more valuable than fellowship with Jesus in His kingdom, one cannot learn from Him.' Our spiritual education depends on the degree of our dedication.

FURTHER STUDY

2 Cor. 4:7–12, 16–18; 6:4–10;
1 Tim. 6:11–16;
2 Tim. 2:1–8

1. How did Paul show he was in a battle?

2. How does Paul encourage Timothy to be a fighter?

Lord Jesus, I understand that You are on a mission, a rescue mission, that will ultimately usher in Your kingdom. By Your grace I am with You. Thank You for Your calling and the strength that You provide to walk with You. Amen.

Upset families

FOR READING & MEDITATION – MATTHEW 10:34–39

*'Do not suppose that I have come to bring peace to the earth.
I did not come to bring peace, but a sword.' (v34)*

Yesterday we highlighted the truth that Jesus never demeaned family loyalties but was emphasising the unrivalled call to Himself. The passage before us today once again reveals something of the drastic and dramatic way in which Jesus upset the normal fabric of domestic life. Because He came as Messiah to establish God's sovereign rule, Jesus will not only bring peace but at times division also. Families will be split in their response to the challenge He brings. Those who become His disciples sometimes find their family members may not understand what they are doing, and may be misunderstood or even rejected by them. Just as Jesus puzzled His own family at times, so His disciples will sometimes baffle and confuse their closest relatives.

FURTHER STUDY

John 15:9–17;
Rom. 15:5–9

1. What is love measured by according to Jesus?

2. Why do we pray for a spirit of unity?

Has responding to His call caused you to be misunderstood, perhaps even disowned, by your family? Take heart. You belong now to a new family – the family of the redeemed – and you may even begin to feel closer to them than you do to your blood relations. Having said that, however, there are sad stories of men and women who, having become Christians and been outlawed by their blood family, found that their new family, the Church, failed to welcome them and give them the nurture and support they needed. This not only grieves the heart of God but surely is far from the picture the New Testament presents of what a loving church family should be. If we do not love our brother whom we can see, says the apostle John, how can we love God whom we cannot see (1 John 4:20)? God forbid that those who lose their families because of their loyalty to Christ should then find the family of God unfriendly and unwelcoming.

Father, forgive us if we are insensitive to the plight of Christians who, because of their loyalty to You, have been rejected by their families. Help us to love and welcome them into their new family. For Your own dear name's sake. Amen.

Next Issue

MAY/JUN 2017

The Promised Holy Spirit

Before His ascension, Jesus made us a promise. His promise was fulfilled on the day of Pentecost when the Holy Spirit came and enabled the first disciples to turn the world upside down. God gives us His same Spirit today.

This issue explores how we can experience the Holy Spirit in our lives – allowing Him to develop our characters, teach us, help us to persevere and enable us to be witnesses. Discover these things, along with other good gifts from the Father, as you consider more about the promised Holy Spirit.

Every Day **with Jesus**

MAY/JUN 2017

The Promised Holy Spirit

'I will pour out my Spirit on all people.'
Joel 2:28

Be revived and refreshed by God's Word   CWR

e   Also available as eBook/ eSubscription

Obtain your copy from CWR, a Christian bookshop or National Distributor.
If you would like to take out a subscription, see the order form at the back of these notes.

Receiving Christ

FOR READING & MEDITATION – MATTHEW 10:40–42

'He who receives you receives me, and he who receives me receives the one who sent me.' (v40)

Here Jesus places great responsibility on those who are unwelcoming to His disciples. 'The way in which people treat you,' He told them, 'is the way they are treating Me.' Dietrich Bonhoeffer, in *The Cost of Discipleship*, said: 'The bearers of Jesus' word receive a final word of promise for their work. They are now Christ's fellow workers and will be like Him in all things. Thus they are to meet those to whom they are sent as if they were Christ Himself. When they are welcomed into a house, Christ enters with them. They are bearers of His presence. They bring with them the most precious gift in all the world, the gift of Jesus Christ.' We are bearers of Christ's presence in our homes, in our church, at school, in our place of work, in the whole world.

FURTHER STUDY

1 Cor. 4:14–17;
1 Thess. 2:1–12;
Heb. 6:10–12;
13:7–8

1. In what ways was Paul a true representative of love?

2. Who is worth imitating?

Some people have taken these words of Jesus and applied them inappropriately. One man, a professing Christian, who was experiencing great difficulty in his family relationships because of his own difficult and demanding behaviour, confronted the members of his family with this text and accused them of being 'Christ crucifiers'. They were deeply offended, as they had no wish to fall foul of the Christian gospel. The reality of the situation was that this man, anxious to cover up his unchristian behaviour, was trying to turn Jesus' statement to his own advantage.

How different is the description in today's verses of a true disciple who shows hospitality to Jesus' servants. Even the smallest act of kindness done in His name will not go unrewarded by Jesus. If we claim the name of Christ, then do we bring the gift of His presence into situations in which we find ourselves?

Lord Jesus, I see that as Your disciple I can bring to people the gift of Your presence. Help me to be conscious of this and truly represent Your love. Help me to be aware also when others bring Your presence to me – and rejoice. Amen.

'Celebrity-ism'

FOR READING & MEDITATION – MATTHEW 19:16–30

'Jesus answered, "If you want to be perfect, go, sell your possessions... Then come, follow me."' (v21)

A new status has appeared amongst us, claims the Christian writer Larry Crabb. That new condition, he says, is 'Celebrity-ism'. He defines it as 'looking up to people just because they are in the public eye'. In today's world, people become celebrities on the flimsiest of pretexts. Jesus, however, was never overawed by the status of those with whom He came into contact. He saw people in their true light, irrespective of their position in life.

The man in our story today who met with Jesus was, we are told, young and rich (v22). He appeared to be honest, respectable and God-fearing. However, he collected commandments in the same way that some people might collect butterflies! Jesus offered to help him to complete his collection by giving him another command: 'Sell your possessions... Then come, follow me' (v21). To his ears those words would have sounded more startling than they do now to ours, as in those days it was generally assumed that people with money, land and prestige were especially blessed by God and were His favourites. They were seen as standing first in line for God's approval.

FURTHER STUDY

Luke 21:1–4;
Col. 1:24–27;
2:9–15;
James 1:9–18

1. What have we been given in Christ?

2. From whom do perfect gifts come?

Characteristically, Jesus turned such an idea on its head by saying that it is as hard for a rich man to enter the kingdom of God as it is for a camel to go through the eye of a needle. In other words, all human ideas about the priority of wealth or fame count for nothing when it comes to entering into the kingdom. He added also that many who are first will be last, and the last will be first (v30). In God's new order there is a reversal of all normal notions of greatness and wealth and fame. Disciples are rich in the things that really matter.

Lord Jesus, how can I thank You enough for transforming my view of life? Help me see clearly now that one thing and one thing alone matters – my relationship with You. Having You I have everything. Thank You my Saviour. Amen.

The first prerequisite

FOR READING & MEDITATION – LUKE 10:38–42

*'but only one thing is needed. Mary has chosen what is better,
and it will not be taken away from her.' (v42)*

Today's reading is one of the best-known incidents in Jesus' life. At one level it shows Jesus' humanity in that He wanted to be with friends, a home to which He could retreat from the pressures of ministry, and 'sisters' who no doubt fussed over Him. But even in this relatively everyday scene, the revolutionary characteristics of the kingdom of God become evident.

In the story, domestic harmony began to fracture when Martha, feeling overburdened by her workload, resented her sister's failure to help. But the issue was not, as is often suggested, an imbalance between the active and the contemplative life, between those that do and those who are quiet before God. A deeper drama was unfolding here. The real scandal was that Mary was behaving like a man! According to the conventions of the time, women were meant to stay in the kitchen. Martha knew her place and kept to it. But Mary did something which was socially risky. For a woman to be at ease in the company of men was regarded in those days as shameless behaviour.

Even more disturbing was the fact that Mary sat at the feet of the teacher. This indicated much more than that she was hanging on Jesus' every word; this was the classic ancient posture of a disciple. It was what you did if you wanted to become a teacher yourself! And Jesus accepted Mary in this stance. Amid all the distracting demands of life, Mary seized the 'kingdom moment' and showed that she wanted more than anything to be a disciple of Jesus.

Let everyone everywhere note that the first prerequisite for being a disciple of Jesus is attentiveness to the Master. Service takes second place to that.

FURTHER STUDY

Deut. 6:4–8;
Mark 12:28–34;
John 21:13–17;
1 John 4:20–21

1. What gives the greatest commandment its significance?

2. How does Jesus link love and service?

Jesus, my Saviour and my God, thank You for reminding me again that what You long for in our relationship is not just service but love. I would put my heart up against Your heart, feel its beat and catch its rhythm. Amen.

FOR READING & MEDITATION – LUKE 11:14–28

'He replied, "Blessed rather are those who hear the word of God and obey it."' (v28)

A mong the crowd who gathered to hear Jesus' life-changing words in today's reading was one woman who, obviously impacted with what He had been saying, suddenly shouted out to Him, 'Blessed is Your mother!' The remark sounded innocent enough, but Jesus responds by saying, 'Blessed rather are those who hear the word of God and obey it.' It was a moment of sentimentality that He could easily have let pass, but J.B. Phillips, in his translation, as a heading for verses 27 and 28, wrote 'Jesus brings sentimentality down to earth'. My dictionary defines sentimentality as 'a mental view coloured by strong emotion'. Following Jesus and being His disciple is much more than sentimental feelings. The stakes are too high for that. He wants lasting disciples who hear and obey God's Word. That's the way to receive true blessing.

FURTHER STUDY

Rom. 6:13–18;
1 Thess.
2:13–16;
2 Thess.
2:13–16; 3:6–10

1. What results from our obedience?

2. How does Paul link the word of men with the Word of God?

I believe it was Oswald Chambers who said that 'sentimentality consists of emotions that you have never worked out in practice or obedience'. How easy it is in Jesus' presence to be 'moved', but 'moved' to what ends? Feelings have to be translated into action, into response. It is a sign of the 'cheap grace' mentioned earlier when people look for an easy ride to heaven.

In their book *Kingdom Ethics*, Glen Stassen and David Gushee put their finger on this problem: 'People congratulate themselves on their being forgiven, without repenting; that God is on their side, without their following in the way of God as revealed in Jesus; that they are Christians, without it making much difference to their lives.' When we respond to His call to true discipleship, we don't just admire Jesus from the sidelines; we follow Him on the road.

Lord Jesus, You make things very clear. Your blessings come to those who do more than just hear Your Word, they obey it also. Your mother was such an example of that. May I be an example too. Amen.

Love and obedience

FOR READING & MEDITATION – JOHN 14:15–31

'I love the Father and... do exactly what my Father has commanded me.' (v31)

In many ways – and this is meant reverently – Jesus Himself is the best model of a disciple we could ever hope to find. He demonstrates in His own relationship with the Father the kind of relationship He longs and hopes for for us.

Jesus was governed by two powerful motivations: love and obedience. Frequently today, love and obedience are regarded by some as incompatible. It is a sign of our times that the pledge to 'love, honour and obey' is absent in many wedding services. It is suggested that to talk about obedience in the marriage ceremony is to confuse issues, because the commitment to love ought to be enough. An old song says, 'Love and marriage, love and marriage, go together like a horse and carriage.' But love and obedience? People seem to have difficulty in tying the two together. Jesus, however, understood obedience as the evidence of love. For Him, love and obedience were joined together by God and should not be put asunder.

FURTHER STUDY

John 16:22–28;
1 Cor. 13:4–7;
Heb. 2:14–3:6

1. How does Jesus model the love Paul talks about?

2. In what ways is Jesus our apostle and high priest?

By acting out the part of a true and loving 'disciple' Jesus, of course, clarified for us what love is all about. Divine love is tender but tough; it both feels and acts, and it blends fierce intensity of emotion with firm commitments. This kind of love is passionate and faithful. It never lets us go or lets us down. It doesn't just utter fine words but expresses itself in self-giving, as demonstrated on the cross. 'The world must learn,' said Jesus, 'that I love the Father like this.' Just as Jesus models a love that is expressed in obedience, we can safely do the same. The surest way to express to the world that we love Jesus is to let them see us following His commandments.

Lord Jesus, just as You demonstrated Your love for Your Father through Your obedience, so may I demonstrate my love for You in the same way. Save me from thinking there can be any other way. Amen.

Long-term obedience

FOR READING & MEDITATION – MATTHEW 28:18–20

'go and make disciples of all nations, baptising them in the name of the Father and of the Son and of the Holy Spirit' (v19)

As we near the end of exploring our call to discipleship, we return to the deep concern that prompted this theme. It is well expressed by Glen Stassen and David Gushee who write: 'When Jesus' way of discipleship is thinned down, marginalised or avoided, the churches and Christians lose their antibodies against infection by secular ideologies that manipulate Christians into serving the purposes of some other lord.'

Today's text forms what we might call the standing-orders or, if you like, the mission statement of the Christian Church. We need to be continually reminded of it. Biblical evangelism is not just a matter of winning people to Christ but of making disciples for Christ. When you think of it, there is no other way the Church can be built up. Imagine the Church without committed disciples, living merely on the vagaries of feelings. Such a movement would have become extinct years ago. Responding to His call means committing ourselves to long-term learning and obedience, whereupon we find ourselves immersed in the glorious love and life of the Trinity – Father, Son and Holy Spirit. Then we embark on the continued teaching and training that makes us mature.

FURTHER STUDY

Eph. 1:17–23; 3:14–21; Col. 1:15–23

1. Immerse yourself in the Trinity life of God as you pray Paul's prayers.

2. About what was the apostle Paul passionate?

Permit once again a personal question: Where do you stand in relation to this mission statement? Are you committed to following Jesus wherever He leads you? Do you enjoy your Christian life and experience, or are you just enduring it? Oswald Chambers, in his characteristic way, said that discipleship is 'personal, passionate devotion to a Person'. Disciples are passionate people whose passion is nurtured by the most passionate Being in the universe.

Lord Jesus, whatever passion I have for You – today I open my heart to receive more of You. Let Your passion ignite my passion. Help me always to receive more of You. In Your peerless and precious name I pray. Amen.

'The Christ Person'

FOR READING & MEDITATION – ACTS 11:25–30

'The disciples were called Christians first at Antioch.' (v26)

We come to our last day of taking a fresh look at the issue of our call to discipleship. In today's reading Barnabas and Saul, seeing the great need of these new disciples at Antioch, 'taught great numbers of people'. Now, as then, new Christians need teaching in the great truths of the gospel and in practical Christ-like living.

It was not enough to profess faith in Christ; converts learnt to demonstrate over time how they were learning to live and behave like Jesus. Decisions were not enough; making disciples was what mattered. So Barnabas and Saul taught the believers in Antioch for a whole year. What a wonderful experience to be taught personally by these great men. These were not just Bible studies for the curious: their teaching was intended to shape the hearers' lives.

FURTHER STUDY

Acts 28:16–24;
28:28–31;
Rom. 16:25–27

1. What is our final glimpse of Paul as a committed disciple?

2. Join Paul in his benediction and give thanks.

Eventually, when those inside the Church had grown to live like Jesus, to act and react in Christ-like ways, then those outside the Church, perhaps rather mockingly or possibly affectionately, started to call them the *Christianos* – the Christ people! Was there something in the lives of these Christians at Antioch that reminded people of the self-giving love of Jesus. Many years ago A.W. Tozer, aware of the trend to water down the claims of Christ in his day, wrote in an article titled 'The Old Cross, and the New' these challenging words: 'God offers life, but not an improved old life. The life He offers is life out of death. It stands always on the far side of the cross.' If at times it feels as if we have failed in our calling, I thank God that, knowing our frailties, He reaches out, takes our hand and calls us further up and further in.

Thank You, Lord Jesus, for what You have taught me about being a true disciple. From this day forward help me to be a more deeply committed follower of You than ever before. For Your honour and glory I pray. Amen.

Order form

4 Easy Ways To Order

1. Phone in your credit card order: **01252 784700** (Mon–Fri, 9.30am – 5pm)
2. Visit our online store at **www.cwr.org.uk/store**
3. Send this form together with your payment to: **CWR, Waverley Abbey House, Waverley Lane, Farnham, Surrey GU9 8EP**
4. Visit a Christian bookshop

For a list of our National Distributors, who supply countries outside the UK, visit **www.cwr.org.uk/distributors**

Your Details (required for orders and donations)

Full Name:	CWR ID No. (if known):
Home Address:	
	Postcode:
Telephone No. (for queries):	Email:

Publications

TITLE	QTY	PRICE	TOTAL
		Total Publications	

UK P&P: up to £24.99 = **£2.99**; £25.00 and over = **FREE**

Elsewhere P&P: up to £10 = **£4.95**; £10.01 – £50 = **£6.95**; £50.01 – £99.99 = **£10**; £100 and over = **£30**

Total Publications and P&P (please allow 14 days for delivery)	A	

All CWR adult Bible reading notes are also available in **eBook** and **email subscription** format. Visit **www.cwr.org.uk** for further information.

Subscriptions* (non direct debit)

	QTY	PRICE (including P&P)			TOTAL
		UK	Europe	Elsewhere	
Every Day with Jesus (1yr, 6 issues)		£15.95	£19.95		
Large Print *Every Day with Jesus* (1yr, 6 issues)		£15.95	£19.95	Please contact nearest National Distributor or CWR direct	
Inspiring Women Every Day (1yr, 6 issues)		£15.95	£19.95		
Life Every Day (Jeff Lucas) (1yr, 6 issues)		£15.95	£19.95		
Mettle: 15–18s (1yr, 3 issues)		£14.50	£16.60		
YP's: 11–14s (1yr, 6 issues)		£15.95	£19.95		
Topz: 7–11s (1yr, 6 issues)		£15.95	£19.95		
Cover to Cover Every Day	Email subscription only, to order visit online store.				
Total Subscriptions (subscription prices already include postage and packing)				B	

Please circle which issue you would like your subscription to commence from:

JAN/FEB   MAR/APR   MAY/JUN   JUL/AUG   SEP/OCT   NOV/DEC   *Mettle* **JAN–APR   MAY–AUG   SEP–DEC**

*Only use this section for subscriptions paid for by credit/debit card or cheque. For Direct Debit subscriptions see overleaf.

We promise to never share your details with other charities. By giving us your personal information, you agree that we may use this to send you information about the ministry of CWR. If you do not want to receive further information by post, please tick here. ☐

Continued overleaf >>

<< See previous page for start of order form

Payment Details

☐ I enclose a cheque/PO made payable to CWR for the amount of: **£** _____

☐ Please charge my credit/debit card.

Cardholder's Name (in BLOCK CAPITALS) _____

Card No. ☐☐☐☐ ☐☐☐☐ ☐☐☐☐ ☐☐☐☐

Expires End ☐☐ ☐☐   Security Code ☐☐☐

Gift to CWR ☐ Please send me an acknowledgement of my gift   **C** [   ]

Gift Aid (your home address required, see overleaf)

giftaid it I am a UK taxpayer and want CWR to reclaim the tax on all my donations for the four years prior to this year **and on** all donations I make from the date of this Gift Aid declaration until further notice.*

Taxpayer's Full Name (in BLOCK CAPITALS) _____

Signature _____   **Date** _____

* I am a UK taxpayer and understand that if I pay less Income Tax and/or Capital Gains Tax than the amount of Gift Aid claimed on all my donations in that tax year it is my responsibility to pay any difference.

GRAND TOTAL (Total of A, B & C)   [   ]

Subscriptions by Direct Debit (UK bank account holders only)

One-year subscriptions cost £15.95 (except *Mettle*: £14.50) and include UK delivery. Please tick relevant boxes and fill in the form below.

☐ *Every Day with Jesus* (1yr, 6 issues)
☐ Large Print *Every Day with Jesus* (1yr, 6 issues)
☐ *Inspiring Women Every Day* (1yr, 6 issues)
☐ *Life Every Day* (Jeff Lucas) (1yr, 6 issues)

☐ *Mettle*: 15–18s (1yr, 3 issues)
☐ *YP's*: 11–14s (1yr, 6 issues)
☐ *Topz*: 7–11s (1yr, 6 issues)

Issue to commence from
☐ Jan/Feb ☐ Jul/Aug   *Mettle* ☐ Jan–Apr
☐ Mar/Apr ☐ Sep/Oct   ☐ May–Aug
☐ May/Jun ☐ Nov/Dec   ☐ Sep–Dec

CWR Instruction to your Bank or Building Society to pay by Direct Debit

DIRECT Debit

Please fill in the form and send to: CWR, Waverley Abbey House, Waverley Lane, Farnham, Surrey GU9 8EP

Name and full postal address of your Bank or Building Society

To: The Manager _____ **Bank/Building Society**

Address _____
_____
_____

Postcode _____

Name(s) of Account Holder(s)
_____

Branch Sort Code
☐☐ ☐☐ ☐☐

Bank/Building Society Account Number
☐☐☐☐☐☐☐☐

Originator's Identification Number

4	2	0	4	8	7

Reference
☐☐☐☐☐☐☐☐☐☐☐☐☐☐☐☐☐☐

Instruction to your Bank or Building Society

Please pay CWR Direct Debits from the account detailed in this Instruction subject to the safeguards assured by the Direct Debit Guarantee.
I understand that this Instruction may remain with CWR and, if so, details will be passed electronically to my Bank/Building Society.

Signature(s)
_____
_____

Date
_____

Banks and Building Societies may not accept Direct Debit Instructions for some types of account